KU-480-124

ACHIEVING QUALITY PERFORMANCE

LESSONS FROM BRITISH INDUSTRY

Edited by

RICHARD TEARE
CYRIL ATKINSON
CLIVE WESTWOOD

CASSELL

HERTFORDSHIRE LIBRARY SERVICE

J M L S	**12/02/97**
	£15.99

Cassell
Villiers House
41/47 Strand
London WC2N 5JE

387 Park Avenue South
New York, NY 10016-8810

© Richard Teare, Cyril Atkinson and Clive Westwood 1994

All rights reserved. No part of this publication
may be reproduced or transmitted in any form or by
any means, electronic or mechanical including
photocopying, recording or any information storage
or retrieval system, without prior permission in
writing from the publishers.

First published 1994
Reprinted 1994

British Library Cataloguing-in-Publication Data
A catalogue record for this book is available from the British Library.

ISBN   0 304 32759 X (hardback)
       0 304 32758 1 (paperback)

Typeset by Fakenham Photosetting Ltd, Fakenham, Norfolk
Printed and bound in Great Britain by Redwood Books, Trowbridge, Wiltshire

CONTENTS

Editors and contributors

EDITORS

Cyril Atkinson is the Executive Director of the National Society for Quality through Teamwork (NSQT) with the challenge of providing continuous support to the Society's members in their strategic development and promoting the culture of quality through teamwork in the UK. He joined the NSQT in 1989 having previously held the position of Vice-President, Quality International, with International Computers Limited (ICL). He has extensive quality management experience with previous senior appointments in design assurance, reliability and manufacturing quality.

Richard Teare is Professor and Associate Head of the Department of Service Industries at Bournemouth University and a non-executive director of the NSQT. He received his Ph.D. in Business Administration from the City University Business School, London, and previously worked for both national and international hotel companies. He is editor of the *International Journal of Contemporary Hospitality Management*, associate editor of the *International Marketing Review* and a member of the Editorial Advisory Board of Strategic Insights into Quality. His publications include five books on aspects of strategic management and marketing in service industries.

Clive Westwood is currently a quality consultant mainly working with the NSQT where he coordinates their conferences, seminars, special events and newsletters. He trained as a production engineer then worked as a unit manager at Mullard Southampton. He then joined Philips, Southampton, as Central Inspection Group Manager, which included responsibility for quality circles and the role of facilitator for the company's total quality culture programme. He is a chartered engineer and a member of the Institute of Electrical Engineers.

CONTRIBUTORS

Alastair Arthur began his career with the Meterological Office at Lerwick Observatory and later transferred into technical and electronic engineering with a varied career in research, design, training, systems development and project management. A graduate of the Open University, he joined a Yorkshire-based defence software engineering firm as development manager, technical consultant and quality manager before moving back to Scotland to take up his present post of Quality Manager with Campbell Lee Computer Services Limited. In this role he is intimately involved with the company's TQM programme, involving quality circles, quality improvement teams and ISO 9001. He is also the current Scottish Co-ordinator for the NSQT.

John F. Chesterton is currently the Quality Improvement Support Manager at ICL Kidsgrove and has been involved in ICL's quality improvement process since its inception in 1986. Additionally, he has forged a reputation in the application of TQM in education. Notable successes include the compilation and delivery of TQM courses for the Careers Research Advisory Centre and involvement with the 'Headteacher into Industry' scheme as well as numerous presentations to schools and colleges country-wide. He has also undertaken cost of quality studies in fields ranging from food processing to microelectronics, using cost of quality as a prime tool to drive profitability and growth in a TQM setting.

John S. A. Edwards received his Ph.D. from the University of Surrey and is currently Sutcliffe Professor of Catering Management in the Department of Service Industries, Bournemouth University. Prior to this he was a Lieutenant-Colonel in the British Army where, over a period of 25 years, he held a number of technical appointments in different regions of the world. Most recently he spent three years in the USA working as a research scientist for the US government. His current research interests focus on the use of food, nutrition and feeding strategies to enhance performance and productivity.

Alan Hodgson was educated at Cambridge University where he received his Ph.D. in Chemistry. He is currently Quality Improvement Manager at Cardiff Laboratories, one of Amersham International's main manufacturing plants in the UK. Since 1988 he has been responsible for the inception and promotion of a quality improvement process at Cardiff, and during this time he developed the 'Training for Quality' programme that helped Cardiff Laboratories win a National Training Award in 1991. His has broad experience in the field of quality improvement and is a regional co-ordinator for the British Deming Society. He is also a regular speaker at conferences both in the UK and for the Juran Institute in the USA.

Tony Ingold trained as a medical microbiologist and received his Ph.D. from the University of London. He was coordinator of the Cancer Clinical Trials Unit, University of Birmingham, and is now Reader in Research at the Birmingham College of Food where he runs a postgraduate Research Unit. He is currently undertaking a major study of productivity in hotels in collaboration with the Hotel & Catering Training Company and the Department of Employment. Other interests include quality improvement and multimedia in education.

Nick Johns is Reader in Hospitality Management at the Hotel School, City College, Norwich, where he has been engaged in teaching and research since 1984. A graduate of the University of Surrey, he received his Ph.D. from Loughborough University. He has written widely on scientific, educational and management topics. His current research interests include quality and productivity management in various operational fields of the hospitality industry.

Tom Kilmartin has 18 years of experience in the hydraulic trade, working in various departments. This experience has enabled him to participate in many quality circle and action team activities, including membership of the 1992 Perkins Award team. He has contributed to a Department of Trade and Industry booklet about quality circles, and he co-authored a paper on total quality management for the Sheet Metal 92 conference held in Birmingham.

Sally J. Messenger has been Lecturer in Hotel Management in the Department of Management Studies for Tourism and Hotel Industries at the University of Surrey since 1989. She has written and co-edited three books, and her particular area of research interest is the management of organizational change applied to education and training in the hospitality industry. Prior to her present post she was Divisional Manager for City and Guilds of London Institute and Accreditation Development Officer for the National Council for Vocational Qualifications.

John Sinclair is Director of the Organizational Change Research Unit at Napier University, Edinburgh. His research and consultancy work has brought him into contact with a wide range of organizations and management teams, particularly with regard to dealing with the problems of planning and managing change. Recent research projects have included empowerment in the workplace and the role of corporate culture, reacting to organizational change and mismanagement within organizations.

John Sparrow Ph.D. is Reader in Human Behaviour and Director for Research at the University of Central England Business School. As a chartered psychologist he has conducted a wide range of research into human behaviour and associated management/policy issues for government, industrial federations and companies. He has published over 50 applied research papers. He acts as a consultant in task, job and work analysis.

Stephen Tanner moved from an academic career after obtaining his Ph.D., and joined the Ford Motor Company in 1978 as a quality engineer specializing in statistical process control and welding destruction testing. In 1985 he moved on to ICL where, as Quality Manager, he was responsible for the first manufacturing plants to receive BSI registration. More recently with Prudential, he has been part of the team which has won a number of awards for its TQM programme. In January 1992 Prudential became the first insurance company to have part of its organization registered by BSI to BS 5750. He frequently gives talks on quality to organizations as diverse as professional conferences and local technical colleges. He was also an invited member on the 1992–3 DTI Quality Roadshow Team and recently trained as a 1993 EFQM assessor.

Alan Woodfield is Managing Director of Hydrapower Dynamics Limited, one of the leading producers of hydraulic hoses used in industry, agriculture, construction, shipping, fighting vehicles and aerospace. He previously held several key positions in the fluid power industry and instigated a management buyout of the company in 1989. He launched a total quality management programme in 1990 and the company won the 1992 Perkins Award in the small company category.

Trevor R. Scott Worthington was educated at Acton College, London, where he received an HNC in Mechanical Engineering. He served his apprenticeship with the Standard Triumph Motor Company and has since gained wide experience in managing quality assurance and control within the British Leyland/Rover Group Company. His experience spans new product quality, calibration, sample approval, quality planning, policies, procedures, inspection instructions, developing traceability controls, conformity of production testing, supplier investigations and product liability. In 1989 he was appointed TQI Manager with responsibility for implementing a total quality improvement programme across the Land Rover site.

Stan Zetie is Senior Lecturer in Operations Management at the University of Central England in Birmingham. A comparatively recent entrant to academe, his previous experience included both line and consulting positions with major British companies such as GKN and British Telecom. His current interests are total quality management, project management and post-experience management education. In the latter context he is responsible for running an in-company Certificate in Management Studies course for Lucas Industries plc.

The companies

Amersham International plc is a leading health science company providing products and services for use in health care, life science research, environmental safety and industrial quality assurance. Amersham has 19 subsidiary companies and a sophisticated international distribution network serving customers throughout the world. Almost 90 per cent of turnover is outside the UK. By working closely with customers, Amersham has helped advance breakthroughs in the clinical diagnosis and treatment of disease, the development of new drugs, the structure and function of DNA and the genetic code. Amersham's technology is also helping to establish higher standards for industrial safety, food and water hygiene and environmental testing.

Campbell Lee Computer Services Limited is a private company based in Falkirk, with branch offices in Paisley and Aberdeen. As both the largest independent software house and IBM 'Business Associate' in Scotland, Campbell Lee is well placed to fulfil its service to Scottish business. The company offers software application solutions to the business problems of its customers, based around the increasingly successful IBM AS/400 computer. An ISO 9001-registered firm, Campbell Lee continues to be one of the pioneer companies to view TQM and ISO 9001 as complementary and not in conflict. Business success is considered inextricably linked to a company ethos of quality of service aimed towards exceeding customer expectations.

Hydrapower Dynamics Limited is one of the leading producers of hydraulic hoses used in industry, agriculture, construction, shipping, fighting vehicles and aerospace. Hydrapower hose assemblies are in use in situations as diverse as the depths of the ocean and outer space. The company is committed to the concept of total quality and maintains BS 5750 (Part 2), ISO 9002 and AQAP (4) quality standards by continuously reviewing systems and procedures to ensure complete customer confidence in the quality of finished products. In this, the aim is to eliminate defects and maintain the highest level of controlled standards.

ICL plc is a leading European-based information technology company with some 26,000 employees and operations in over 70 countries worldwide. It has a successful strategy of growth through investment in research and development, partnerships and joint ventures. In 1991 ICL's revenue increased by 16 per cent to £1,876 million (US$3.3 billion). A technological leader and supplier of high-quality services and products, ICL was one of the first companies worldwide to have its entire range of products conforming to open standards.

Prudential Corporation plc is one of the world's largest and strongest financial services groups. Its main businesses are life insurance and pensions, general insurance, life and general reinsurance and investment management. In the UK, the organization is dominated by the Home Service Division whose core products are life assurance, personal pensions and general insurance. The field force of some 13,000 local representatives is supported by Life Administration offices in Reading and Belfast where some 1,500 people work. Established in 1848, by 1991 Prudential had 15 million contract records, processed on average 100,000 new proposals each month and received more than £6 billion in premium income from long-term business.

Rover Group plc is Britain's largest motor manufacturer, producing half a million vehicles a year. The group designs, manufactures and markets cars in the small, medium and executive sectors, car-derived vans and specialist four-wheel-drive vehicles. The Rover Group, with annual sales of £3,700 million and exports of over £1,100 million, is the UK's leading car producer and exporter, selling its vehicles in 150 markets worldwide. Land Rover is the marque name for the company's world-famous four-wheel-drive vehicle. The Solihull site employs 8,000 people in designing, manufacturing and assembling its own engines, gearboxes, axles, bodies, paints and trims, and in the assembly of the complete Defender, Discovery and Range Rover vehicles.

The National Society for Quality through Teamwork

'Continuous improvement' is a phrase which is quite common in the language of the management philosophy gurus. The concept is as old as the hills, although Darwin more recently described it in terms of 'natural selection'. The National Society for Quality through Teamwork (NSQT) was founded as a result of a few UK companies realizing that natural selection – the elimination of the weak – would apply to them if they did not create a climate of continuous improvement inside their businesses and, in so doing, become more competitive. The few, aided by a small number of UK consultants, sought ideas from the main global challengers in the 1970s, namely the Japanese. They identified a particular form of teamworking which the Japanese had adopted and which they called 'quality control circles'. The guidelines for this method of working appeared straightforward, and an easy transfer of the concept was anticipated.

By the end of the 1970s, it had become clear that there was much more to the idea of involving people in continuous improvement than was first envisaged, and the few companies attempting the transfer formed the Society as a result. The initial focus related to the philosophy of quality control circles, known more commonly in the western world as just 'quality circles'. The Society's aim was, and still is, to encourage mutual support of member companies who are seeking to enhance their business by utilizing the creative ability of their total workforce. Additionally, the Society endeavours to assist and support companies wishing to explore the opportunities available to them in the people-involvement field. In this, the NSQT provides facilitation to management teams so that they evolve the best possible continuous improvement programme; training in implementation for managers and their staff; conferences and workshops to expand understanding and awareness; and regular networking meetings throughout the UK.

A major development has been the introduction of award schemes which are designed to provide the UK business world with an opportunity to benchmark: that is, to compare themselves against the 'best in class'. The Perkins Award, a scheme sponsored by Perkins Engines, began in 1987. Initially, the aim was to recognize the organization which gave the best support to, and improvement in, its quality circle programme. In this, the judges had to take into account each company's circumstances so that a level playing field would exist and only commitment, systems and people involvement would count. The Perkins Award has since moved closer to the American Malcolm Baldridge Award and the European Quality Award, but the emphasis remains on the goal of achieving maximum employee involvement in the context of what is now commonly referred to as a total quality management programme. In 1992 the award was extended by introducing categories for large and small companies, won by Land Rover and Hydrapower Dynamics respectively. All six finalists are featured in this book, and it is hoped that their efforts will inspire other UK businesses to begin or continue a fruitful and continuous improvement journey.

Recognition of achievement and benchmarking against the best are two of the NSQT's key ingredients for change. The Perkins Award and, in recent years, the awards sponsored by Michelin and Wedgwood meet both of these needs.

The National Society for Quality through Teamwork is a registered charity dedicated to enabling companies in all sectors of British Industry to achieve their goals in continuous improvement, people involvement and customer service. NSQT member organizations represent many different industries and vary in size from small, regionally based companies to major multinationals. For membership information, write to the NSQT at 2 Castle Street, Salisbury SP1 1BB.

Foreword

As sponsors, with the National Society for Quality through Teamwork, of the Perkins Award, we are very pleased that this book commits to record the achievements of the participating companies in the 1992 event. All of these enterprises have demonstrated, in different ways, their commitment to quality through teamwork and the subsequent effect upon their organizations.

As a diesel design, manufacturing and service company, Perkins has a long tradition and reputation for quality. In recent years, however, we have recognized the strategic need for a total approach to every aspect of the business.

The company has embarked on this process of continuous improvement in everything it does, aiming to delight our customers, be they internal to the organization or external purchasers of our output of goods and services across the world.

The total quality programme is now in its third year, and today we have over 500 working teams throughout the group which are engaged upon change for improvement in our organization.

Many of these teams have customer representatives working as members. Other teams include staff from suppliers. Where necessary these external participants have completed the Perkins training programme.

All of this is part of our journey towards total quality along the road of continuous improvement. It began in 1990 with a training programme which included every one of our 3,500 employees throughout the world.

The programme was designed for Perkins by Quest Consultancy, which conducted the early training. This training included 30 employees, selected as facilitators from all areas of the business, whose role was then to extend the initial training to the remaining management, staff and factory employees. Since TQ was introduced at Perkins, over 20,000 working days of training have been invested in the programme.

Once trained, our employees have enthusiastically responded to the opportunity to improve their own processes, and recent surveys have confirmed this enthusiasm and the wish to participate in further improvement programmes. The total quality approach, by focusing on processes and bringing together representatives or process owners is fundamentally changing the way our organization works, crossing functional responsibility boundaries and acting directly upon the process flow towards the customer.

Many employees are finding that, as a result of this teamwork, they now have a chance to exercise new creative energy in their jobs. In addition, by working in teams on projects, employees are gaining a wider view of their role in sometimes extended process chains. These are powerful stimuli for group and personal satisfaction, and the source for further motivation and involvement.

In the business context, Perkins has set priority areas for improvement and all employees are encouraged to contribute towards these within their own department, section or process. In Peterborough Engines, the largest business within the Perkins Group, these have been defined as follows:

> Zero defects
> Quicker/better   } in everything
> Reduced cost   } that we do
> 100% involvement

Every one of these goals is ultimately focused on the customer. By aiming to exceed our customers' expectations as a result of our efforts towards these goals, Perkins is confident of future growth.

Teamwork is the driving force for improvement and change – and change is now recognized as an essential element in the continuance of Perkins' success. Perkins is committed through change processes to offer competitive products and services, developing at an even faster rate to outpace competition and attract new customers.

In the United Kingdom, now beginning to recognize the importance of competitive wealth creation, the Perkins Award is an encouragement to organizations wishing to promote improvement, which seek the means to compare themselves to others with the same ambition. From the number and diversity of entries, it is clear that the movement is strengthening every year. This is one of the really rewarding aspects of the award, which will ensure its continuation.

Previous winners, Land Rover and Hydrapower, have demonstrated powerfully the positive impact on their business brought about by quality and teamworking initiatives. Equally, Hewlett Packard, and Michelin – also previous holders of the award – are showing the way to move industry forward.

Myles Coleman, General Manager – Manufacturing, Perkins Engines
June 1993

Preface

Total quality management has become the management philosophy of the 1990s, but as yet there are few management texts which focus on the complex practicalities associated with designing and implementing a quality improvement programme with the aim of achieving better quality performance. This is a crucially important topic which is best dealt with by way of quality improvement illustrations documenting why, how and what action is needed to improve manufacturing/service performance.

Achieving Quality Performance aims to provide detailed examples of quality improvement programmes devised by six award-winning British companies. In essence, the book poses a fundamental question which is a common theme throughout: 'How do we involve all the people in our organization in quality improvement?' Each of the featured companies was a national finalist in the 1992 Perkins Award organized by the National Society for Quality through Teamwork (NSQT) and sponsored by Perkins Engines, Peterborough. The companies featured are: Amersham International; Campbell Lee Computer Services; Hydrapower Dynamics; ICL (Kidsgrove Manufacturing Operations); Land Rover; and Prudential Assurance.

Each chapter is structured so as to provide an introduction to the company, the aims of its quality improvement programme, a detailed account of how quality improvement was achieved and a review of the implications arising. Among the key issues addressed by each company are the following:

- Quality improvement strategy, structure plans and mission within the company.
- Visible management commitment to the quality improvement programme.
- Measurement to control and adjust the programme.
- Related training provision at all levels in the company.
- Innovation.
- Problem identification and correction.
- Recognition of achievements.
- Learning from failures.
- Involvement of all members of the organization.

This book would not have been possible without the enthusiastic support of the featured companies and we sincerely thank them, and the team of contributors who have worked so hard to replay in a dynamic, realistic way the quality improvement challenges that the companies are addressing. We would also like to thank Steve Cook, Roz Hopkins and Peter Harrison (Cassell), David Royle and Chris Bessant.

Richard Teare, Cyril Atkinson, Clive Westwood
September 1993

ONE

AMERSHAM INTERNATIONAL PLC:
Stimulating participation in quality improvement

JOHN EDWARDS
AND
ALAN HODGSON

ONE

Amersham International plc:
Stimulating participation in quality improvement

INTRODUCTION

The commitment to quality improvement in any organization must be total. It is not a short-term phenomenon, but a long-term investment which requires adequate resources; above all, it demands a commitment to the process at all levels. Securing the involvement of individuals is the central theme of the quality improvement process at Amersham International's Cardiff Laboratories, where the goal is the elusive one of total participation. A complementary theme is continuous improvement achieved step by step, project by project. Together these themes have been used so that, each year, more and more of the workforce are drawn into numerous projects, thereby increasing participation.

AMERSHAM INTERNATIONAL PLC

Amersham International plc is a leading health science company specializing in the development, manufacture and distribution of radioactive and non-radioactive products and services worldwide (Figure 1.1). It has earned for itself a reputation for safety, integrity and precision in the handling and international distribution of radioactive and non-radioactive products using technology that has been developed over the last 50 years. There are 19 subsidiary companies throughout the world and almost 90 per cent of its turnover is abroad. It exports to almost every country in the world and employs, in the UK, some 1,600 people. Its principal UK production facilities are located at Amersham and Cardiff.

Organization

Amersham's resources and expertise are organized and focused into three distinct areas:

Facts:
19 overseas subsidiaries
Customers in 150 countries
Manufacturing facilities in Europe and USA
3 principal manufacturing sites in UK: Amersham, Cardiff and Gloucester

Figure 1.1   Amersham International plc: organization

- *Health care*   'Unique products for the early diagnosis and treatment of illness and disease.'
- *Life science*   'Specialized products and technologies designed to investigate and help explain the fundamental processes of living cells in order to understand disease and develop better ways of controlling and combating it.'
- *Industrial quality and safety assurance*   'Sealed sources used in precision gauging and non-destructive testing for quality and safety assurance applications in industry, as well as biochemical assays for the detection of environmental pollutants and microbial contamination in food and water.'

Manufacturing mission and strategy

The manufacturing mission at Cardiff Laboratories is twofold:

- To manufacture safely or to supply the required quantity of products both in volume and in type required by the customer, to the quality specification, the specific cost of manufacture and the agreed schedule.
- To manufacture right first time, every time, with minimum waste, and to seek to improve continuously the effectiveness and cost efficiency of the total operation.

In order to achieve this mission, the strategy is to focus on best manufacturing practices and the principles of total quality. A 'Manufacturing Excellence Programme' supported by a site-wide total quality process is the mechanism for achieving this. These aim to establish the following:

- Best manufacturing methods.
- A culture change, moving from a research-based establishment to that of a professional manufacturing organization.
- The principles of total quality in all areas of the site and at all levels.

BACKGROUND TO THE QUALITY IMPROVEMENT PROGRAMME

In early 1988 Amersham's Cardiff site began to focus increasingly on quality improvement. The company's original strength was founded and built upon its position in scientific research. While the company wished to retain this, it perceived a require-ment to change the organizational focus and culture by incorporating and building up its ability and reputation for manufacturing excellence. The ultimate aim was to achieve world-class status in quality by adopting the principles captured in the 'quality policy' (Figure 1.2), namely:

- Cardiff Manufacturing will be seen by its competitors and cus-tomers as a world-class leader in quality.
- We will make quality and safety key priorities in everything we do.
- We will fully understand the needs of our internal and external customers, and supply products and services that meet or exceed their expectations.
- We will use everyone's skills and enthusiasm to achieve our qual-ity policy.
- As part of our quality improvement approach to manufacturing, Cardiff Manufacturing quality council will set annual, ongoing targets for quality improvement based on the principle of 'get it right first time'.

Figure 1.2 Cardiff Manufacturing quality policy

- To seek excellence.
- To delight the customer.
- To gain total involvement.
- To set revolutionary targets.

The Manufacturing Excellence Programme began in 1989 and had as its key focus three aims:

- Reliability.
- Predictability.
- Consistency and the relentless desire to do better.

One of the business groups successfully pioneered a pilot programme and, following company reorganization in late 1990, the programme was scaled up and adopted at Cardiff Laboratories.

Cardiff Laboratories took as its model for quality improvement the work of Dr Joseph Juran. In his review of world-class organizations in the USA (Juran, 1991) one of his recommendations was that the supporting infrastructure should be in place before more widespread involvement is sought. Only in this way could the long-term and enduring participation of all those involved be secured.

The introduction of quality improvement was planned using a four-phase approach. Although overlap between the phases was inevitable, the order of implementation was considered and subsequently established as being absolutely critical. The phases involved were as follows:

- *Phase 1: Providing the vision*
  Awareness training
  The four stages of quality

- *Phase 2: Management action*
  The 'vital few' projects
  Training for quality
  Quality councils
  The quality champion

- *Phase 3: Increasing the participation*
  Quality circles
  Quality action teams
  Facilitators
  Recognition
  Rewards
  New skills

- *Phase 4: Business alignment*
  Department purpose analysis
  Benchmarking
  ISO 9002

PHASE 1: PROVIDING THE VISION

The first step in quality leadership is to provide a vision for the future. The vision is essential to the success of the process, but it has to be one that will excite and inspire people; something that individuals can 'buy into'. The key then is to sell that vision to everybody.

Ideas for the vision can come from a number of places. They can come, for example, from learning about the success of other companies; or simply from dreaming about what things might be like if everything worked perfectly. Cardiff Laboratories used the manufacturing mission as its vision, and to win people over it adopted awareness training and a planning tool called the 'four stages of quality'.

Awareness training

In 1988 quality improvement was a comparatively new concept to most people. The immediate aim, therefore, was to introduce this new concept and the ideas surrounding it to everybody. The overall aim was to get people to change by teaching them how to do things differently from the way they did them before – 'training for quality'. A comprehensive training package was developed, details of which are given in Table 1.1.

Training began with awareness briefing sessions for everybody. The immediate response was enthusiastic. However, it soon became obvious from feedback being

Table 1.1   Training for quality

	Year commenced	Training	Time involved
Phase 1	1988	Introduction to quality	1 hour
	1990	The quality advantage	1 day
Phase 2		Juran for managing quality	Ongoing
	1988	The problem-solving process	2 days
	1989	On-the-job reinforcement	Weeks
Phase 3	1991	Broadening the skills	
		Understanding variations using SPC	
		Experimental design and Taguchi methods	
		FMEA	
		IE methods	
		Kepner Tregoe	
		Quality function deployment	

received that more than a first session would be necessary if any degree of commit-ment or level of progress was to be sustained.

In 1990 the entire workforce was given the opportunity to attend a comprehensive one-day course called 'The Quality Advantage'. This course followed up and built on the initial briefings by helping to reinforce the themes of continuous improvement and total involvement. The success of the course was measured by surveying participants. The overall score obtained was 73 per cent, providing a ranking between good and very good.

During the awareness training it became apparent that the quality programme could not overgeneralize and would need to be more specific than originally thought. People were asking the question: 'What does it mean for me in my area?' In answering this question, the 'four stages of quality' were developed at Cardiff, and they turned out to be among the most important of all the planning tools.

The four stages of quality

In the four stages of quality, each functional area is asked to define the key quality success factors in its contribution towards the overall business. Then, for each factor, it must define what excellence would mean. This stage in quality development is called 'world class'.

As a guide to setting the targets, three other stages are used and these are shown in Table 1.2. At each of these stages, functional areas specify what targets are to be met on the road to 'world class'.

The four stages of quality were found to be invaluable in converting general statements into real, understandable targets for each area. Some of the examples used are given in Table 1.3. This not only helped people to understand exactly what was involved, but also convinced many of the benefits of quality. It led some to wonder why a programme such as this had not been started many years earlier.

Table 1.2   The four stages of quality

Stage 1 Innocence	Stage 2 Awakening	Stage 3 Commitment and Implementation	Stage 4 World class
1. Repeats 2. Errors 3. Apologies	10% reduction	50% reduction	1. Right first time 2. Zero defects 3. Total customer satisfaction

Table 1.3   The four stages of quality: examples

Stage 1 Innocence	Stage 2 Awakening	Stage 3 Commitment	Stage 4 World class
Manufacturing Process failures at 30%	Failures reduced to 20%	Failures reduced to 10%	No process failures
Safety Can only have tidy lab if we do no work	Defects down 10% using zero defect standard	Defects down 60%	No housekeeping defects
Finance Give them the same reports we have always given	Consult with users to define reporting requirements	75% of systems improved to meet requirements	100% of systems fully meet users' requirements

PHASE 2: MANAGEMENT ACTION

Having provided individuals with the vision, the company then had to demonstrate that things could be made to happen. Only by adopting this approach could it convince others to take part. Four specific areas were addressed to provide the evidence and help to get the quality message across.

The 'vital few' projects

If total involvement was to mean anything, it was considered essential that it started with, and included, managers. It was important for them to take part in quality improvement projects, first to set an example, and second to ensure that the problems were solved. These problems were, after all, the ones that had considerable financial implications.

The original process was begun by managers addressing and attacking the 'vital few' problems. The original quality improvement project teams focused on major cross-functional problems such as the handover of newly developed products, safety attitudes and essential savings. The projects often took 12 months or more to identify causes and to prove that a breakthrough had been achieved.

Thereafter, the next range of projects was approached under the banner of manufacturing excellence. Some of these took even longer and many of them are still ongoing today. Examples of these projects include scheduling of manufacturing projects, forecasting and pack-size rationalization.

The aim has been to get all managers involved in quality improvement projects. Dr Juran provided some guidelines at a conference in London in 1990. His experience showed that, if only 20 per cent of managers are involved in projects, an evolutionary rate is indicated; whereas 80 per cent or more denotes a revolutionary rate. With over 50 major projects completed since 1988, 100 per cent involvement by senior and middle management has been achieved.

Training for quality

Training for quality was used to teach people how to approach and undertake their jobs differently. By building on the original awareness sessions in Phase 1, a versatile package (Table 1.1) was instituted with the following aims:

* To develop team problem-solving skills in project team leaders.
* To develop individual problem-solving skills to enable successful participation in quality circles and quality action teams.

This stage turned out to be the key phase of the training programme, converting enthusiasm developed during the awareness training into solid results. Again, another in-house programme was developed for potential project leaders. They were introduced to the classic problem-solving techniques in a four-step process:

* FOCUS on a problem.
* ANALYSE the problem.
* DEVELOP a solution.
* EXECUTE the implementation plan.

Since 1988, 130 participants have attended the courses, and post-course surveys have given an average rating of 78 per cent. Over 80 per cent of course participants have subsequently gone on to lead or take part in quality circles or quality action teams.

The trainees next had to find volunteers from the workplace to work in quality circles and quality action teams. Having done this, they selected real problems to work on in order to practise and gain experience of the process. Projects normally lasted several weeks with the leaders acting as trainers to the rest of the team, but with a facilitator being on hand to help out where necessary.

Quality councils

In order for management to demonstrate its commitment to the quality improvement process, a quality council concept was adopted. This provided the high visibility needed, since management action could then be used as a means of promoting, coordinating and institutionalizing quality improvement activities.

The original Quality Council was established in 1988 and since then it has developed and adapted to meet the changes resulting from company reorganization. In 1990 it was renamed and restructured to become the Cardiff Manufacturing Quality Council with responsibilities for the production groups on site, representing approximately 65 per cent of the workforce. In 1991 it was enlarged to embrace the administrative, site engineering and site services groups. In 1992 the quality council was complete when the development division joined, making 100 per cent participation. In addition, the manufacturing group at Gloucester is also represented on the council.

The quality council is now chaired by the site director and includes senior site managers and the facilitator group. It meets monthly with the following aims:

- To decide strategy.
- To review progress.
- To agree training.
- To agree the award system and organize recognition events.

The quality champion

In the early stages it was found to be vital to have someone concentrating 100 per cent on quality. In addition to having one person in the facilitator role, there was so much learning to do and only a full-time individual could devote the time needed. However, it came to be seen that quality improvements were happening only through a 'quality champion'. While managers would give their wholehearted support, the champion was seen as the person to make things happen. This took the onus away from individuals becoming directly involved and removed ownership of the processes or ideas. To avoid this, champions must work constantly to hand over more and more responsibility to line managers and to make their original roles unnecessary.

PHASE 3: INCREASING THE PARTICIPATION

Once the supporting infrastructure was in place, the matter of how and when to increase participation could be considered. The first problem was to decide exactly when to start. This was solved by the workforce themselves. There was an enthusiastic demand for involvement, with people from all areas volunteering to take part. The aim was to move gradually from the 'vital few' problems to the 'useful many' and, in doing so, to involve more and more of the workforce. This was achieved by calling on a number of techniques.

Quality circles

In classical quality circles, volunteers from the same area select and solve their own problems. Starting on a trial basis – thinking big, but starting small – an area was chosen where enthusiasm was high. Step by step, people joined in when it was discovered what did and what did not work well. For example, it was established that quality circles worked best without the local section manager. Under these circumstances, members felt less inhibited in raising and discussing problems.

This worked well in the early stages, but caused problems later on. Some managers were very proactive in taking an interest and encouraging quality circles. Others felt excluded, were uncertain about how to give support, and inevitably left it to the facilitator. The facilitator needed to be aware of this and had to be prepared to stand back and encourage the line manager to become involved.

Quality action teams

As more experience was gained, many groups began to shift to looking at local customer and supplier issues in cross-functional groups. In order to differentiate the cross-functional aspects, the new groups were called quality action teams.

Quality action teams are similar to quality circles, many being composed of volunteers who decide for themselves what problems to address. Others have their projects and leaders selected by managers. In these cases the leader seeks volunteers to join the team. For the major projects, of course, the team leader and members are usually chosen by the senior management.

Over time, quality circles and quality action teams have become the main vehicles for stimulating participation. They have proved to be a great success: since the launch of the quality improvement process, Cardiff Laboratories has started over 200 projects.

Facilitators

Originally, one facilitator was used to launch quality circles. The Cardiff workforce is generally enthusiastic and well educated (50 per cent have professional qualifications) and it was found that people adapted easily to the change process. Indeed, the ease with which they adapted was mistakenly taken to show that they required little or even no support. Although good results continued to be produced by the quality circles and quality action teams, there were signs that the process was not always effectively and efficiently followed.

It was decided to establish and achieve further progress by using a number of part-time facilitators. They were nominated by line management, to include middle management, but they continued to report through the normal chain. Their responsibilities evolved and developed until they were guiding projects in their own areas and promoting cross-functional communications. Facilitators worked constantly to hand more and more responsibility over to line managers and so make their original roles unnecessary.

Recognition

It took the experience of three or four projects before people changed the way they worked and started to adopt an instinctive quality behaviour – the real culture change. Accordingly, everybody was encouraged to commit themselves to project-by-project

CASE STUDY 1
PRODUCTION QUALITY CIRCLE

A quality circle in one of the production sections called themselves the 'Tacklers'. They drew the flow of work in their area on a flow chart and then brainstormed for problems at each stage. They identified 117 issues of which 52 per cent were agreed to be within their control. By using a selection grid, the circle ranked these into a list of priorities for action. For their first project they chose one they judged to be the easiest to solve. They concluded the FOCUS phase by defining the project simply as: 'Location: Is it where it should be? Our aim is everything in its right place.'

The ANALYSE phase began with data collection to find the extent of the problem. This showed that the section lost over three hours a week looking for essential items in the laboratory. Pareto analysis clearly showed the location of equipment to be the greatest problem, and this is where the quality circle concentrated its efforts.

Their laboratory area included many different types of equipment, but they agreed to use pipettes as the test case of the project (pipettes are hand-held instruments that accurately dispense volumes of fluid, in this case very small volumes, such as 50 micro-litres, which is equivalent to one-hundredth of the dose given by a medicine spoon). By using a fishbone diagram, the circle identified likely causes of the pipettes not being in their correct locations. They summarized these causes as follows:

- Nobody responsible.
- Items now replaced.
- No logging system.
- No specific locations.
- Failures not repaired.

They launched into the DEVELOP phase by seeking innovative solutions, again using brainstorming. They decided to try colour coding:

- To identify ownership.
- To specify locations.
- To reduce movement between areas.

Each area of the laboratory was designated a colour and pipettes were coloured accordingly. The system also allowed misplaced pipettes to be easily identified.

The solution was implemented and monitored in the EXECUTE phase. The first audit brought disappointing results – several pipettes were found in the wrong locations. With renewed determination they searched for the reason and pointed the finger at broken pipettes. Anyone finding a broken or unusable pipette immediately borrowed one from another area, but neglected to return it. This time the solution was to collect and repair all the pipettes and then allocate a working set to everyone. A system for repairing future breakages was also introduced.

It was a relief when the next monitoring audit showed all pipettes in correct locations – zero defects – and this was maintained for the following 10 audits. With this problem cracked, the quality circle moved on to the remaining equipment and adapted the colour-coding approach as necessary.

Over a year later, they repeated their original data collection and were delighted to find that the time lost by the section in looking for equipment had been reduced by 98 per cent with overall loss of time down by 80 per cent. In addition, the number of pipettes needed in the area was reduced by 75 per cent, a major cost avoidance of over £10,000 as future purchases became unnecessary. The work of the quality circle showed that problems in an area are best solved by the people working there – when the ownership is theirs.

CASE STUDY 2
PRODUCTION QUALITY CIRCLE

A quality circle in another production area brainstormed for problems and listed over 70 items over which they had varying degrees of control. These were reduced to 13 items to be ranked according to ease of solving, availability of data, cost of quality, and hassle. The quality circle's first project was chosen from halfway down the list. It was one they all felt keenest to work on: availability of equipment.

Several members were uncertain at this stage about using the problem-solving process because they thought they knew the solution. In their opinion, equipment was in short supply because of inadequate expenditure – buy more equipment and the problem would be solved. However, they were persuaded to be patient and use the process. This was fortunate because the cause (and solution) turned out to be completely different.

The first ANALYSE step was to find the extent of the problem by data collection. A three-pronged approach was adopted:

- A questionnaire was used to identify commonly unavailable equipment.
- An audit was made of the number of specific items that could be found in the area.
- A survey was to find the 'ideal world' number of pieces of equipment needed.

Data from the questionnaire showed that 'monitors' caused some of the largest problems, so the circle decided to focus on these. Monitors are electrical instruments used for detecting radiation and comprise a body the size of a small tissue box with a detachable detector connected by cable.

The data showed that there were indeed fewer monitors in the laboratory than the ideal – so more were eventually purchased. But the shortfall seemed too small (5 per cent) to explain the poor availability. So the circle resorted to using a fishbone diagram to identify causes. During this listing of causes, it gradually emerged that several were related to breakages. Further investigation showed £12,000 was being spent annually on repairing broken monitors, and that many of the monitors uncovered in the original survey were 'broken awaiting repair', i.e. not available for use. Poor availability was therefore directly caused by the high level of breakages.

It is interesting to note that the original 'gut feeling' solution of simply buying more monitors would not have solved the problem – but it could have increased breakages and repair costs, and left availability unaffected.

The quality circle then quickly moved on to discover the main cause of breakages using another fishbone diagram. They soon agreed the primary cause: they all tended to perch the monitors in unstable positions during and between use. As a consequence, they were easily and frequently knocked over and broken.

With the true cause identified, the DEVELOP and EXECUTE phases were more straight-forward. The quality circle designed a special clip to hold the monitors during and between use at the workplace – it provided a stable location and allowed easy manipulation. In fact, it was more convenient all round.

The result was a saving of nearly all the £12,000 of repair costs and something close to 100 per cent availability of monitors. But a more important outcome was the lesson that jumping to conclusions does not give a quality result.

improvement. This was achieved by giving recognition to involvement and success, whenever and wherever possible. Care had to be taken not to 'hype' the participation process, which was found to lead to cynicism and unrealistic expectations. Juran warns against the danger of simply becoming a cheer-leader instead of a real leader. A similar message is given by Dr W. Edwards Deming: 'Eliminate the use of slogans, posters and exhortations . . . without providing methods' (Deming, 1986).

CASE STUDY 3
CROSS-FUNCTIONAL QUALITY ACTION TEAM

One of the newer products was troubled not only by significant batch-to-batch variation but also, more worryingly, by within-batch variation. The product comprises a series of components provided in solution in bottles. When these components are used according to the protocol provided with the product, a consistent result is expected – in fact, it is guaranteed in the product specifications. So this variation was not only increasing production costs but was jeopardizing sales of £1 million.

A multifunctional quality action team was established with representatives from production, process development and R & D, and with contact being maintained with marketing colleagues. The aim was to make the product more robust, both in-house and in the customer's hands. The team moved straight into the ANALYSE phase by reviewing previous attempts to improve the production process. These had used a hit-and-miss approach of investigating one possibly important factor at a time. The team decided that a more effective approach was needed, and chose this time to try Taguchi methods of experimental design.

They brainstormed, agreed the critical factors in the production process and decided different levels over which to test them. They then designed experiments (using a Taguchi orthogonal array) to prove the causes. Disappointingly, all their theories were unsuccessful as none of the factors tested was shown to have a significant affect on the variability.

They next turned their attention to the protocol for using the product, which was also used for in-house testing. Again they brainstormed for the critical factors (and test limits) and designed another orthogonal array of experiments. Success! On this occasion two factors were shown to be the main culprits. This meant that the recommended methods of testing and using the product were introducing the variation.

The experiments also showed the best combination of factors to minimize variation, so it was a simple task to change the protocol for in-house and customer use. Part of the EXECUTE phase also seeks to 'hold the gains' and prevent recurrence. To this end, the quality action team developed a statistical process control chart to monitor future batches. This shows the reduction in variation after the change, and also new control limits for monitoring future batches.

Overall, the project had the following results:

- It secured sales of a £1 million product.
- It reduced quality control costs by 90 per cent.
- It put a more predictable product in the customer's hands.

It also showed that these new techniques can be valuable in project work, especially on product-related problems.

To provide the recognition required, Cardiff Laboratories has adopted a number of methods:

- An annual quality day in November has been organized for the past three years and used as the celebration of quality successes. In 1991 this took the format of an exhibition of project work undertaken by over 30 quality circles and quality action teams. Colleagues and friends from industry, academia and the local community joined the 350 people (75 per cent of the site) who visited the exhibition at the Cardiff site.
- Poster displays of completed projects are used to promote achievements. These

CASE STUDY 4
MANAGEMENT-SPONSORED QUALITY ACTION TEAM

Senior staff and managers also serve on quality action teams looking at the major issues, the 'vital few' problems. One such team revolutionized the supply of glass vials – the main container for a major product range. Traditionally, vials had always been washed before use at a cost of £155,000 per annum. The quality action team was given the brief of reducing this cost but, to complicate matters, no one had any hard facts about why the original decision to wash vials was taken.

Several theories existed and these were used in the ANALYSE phase to build up a fishbone diagram of likely reasons for the decision. The most strongly held view was that 'silicate ions would be dissolved from the glass surface by using our solvents in unwashed vials'. Another was that 'the production process introduces grease into the vials'. All the most likely causes were investigated by a variety of data collection methods, including the following:

- Conductivity tests for dissolved ions.
- Visual inspection of vials before washing.
- Consulting experts, e.g. Pilkingtons in the glass business.

Most of the theories were wrong: washing vials made no difference to conductivity tests. There was no evidence for grease, but there was evidence for dust particles in some of the vials. This contamination seemed to occur during storage because some vials were stored for up to six months before use. When the question 'why?' was asked, it emerged that the supplier would only send six months' supply in a single shipment. Although the vials were received covered, the protection was not robust and was often damaged or lost during storage and movement in the warehouse.

At last, the team felt it was on the right track and so moved to the DEVELOP phase to look for solutions. It decided to seek a supplier who would ship more frequently, and who could guarantee cleanliness in production and protection in shipping.

With the help of a purchasing colleague co-opted on to the team, such a supplier (already used by the company) was identified and visited. The team was convinced by the visit, where they saw vials being shrink-wrapped in small batches in a clean room after production. The supplier was also willing to ship monthly.

But the project was not over yet: more work had to be done in the DEVELOP and EXECUTE phases to ensure success. Batches of vials were received for trial in the dispensing operation and were used unwashed with test products. These were analysed over the next six months and showed no problems. So the supplier was changed and washing became a thing of the past – the company no longer did something just because it had always been done. The new supplier was also cheaper than the original and this, along with other small savings, helped the project to save £180,000 annually.

are designed by the quality circles and action teams themselves and many adorn the corridor of the main building at Cardiff Laboratories.

- A newsletter, *Quality Circular*, has played its part in publicizing involvement and success. Wherever possible, articles for publication are written by the project groups themselves.
- Each month a quality circle or quality action team presents its results to the quality council and this forms the first topic of the monthly agenda. Similarly, teams will brief other senior management and company executives – for example, the manufacturing director, chief executive or chairman – when they visit the Cardiff site.

- One quality circle gave a presentation at the Total Quality Users' Convention in London in 1991, thereby providing valuable recognition for the participants.
- The quality improvement manager gave presentations at the Juran Institute's annual convention in Atlanta in 1991 and Chicago in 1992. Since 1982 the Juran Institute in the USA has been holding an annual convention with invited guest speakers from around the world.

Finding new and innovative ways of publicizing people's successes is an ongoing responsibility of any quality improvement drive, but once started along this route it is difficult to stop. People were asked what would convince them of the company's commitment to quality. The most common response was 'Mentioning it in the regular monthly team briefing would make it official.' When asked what would give them the message that interest had been lost, the most common reply was 'When you stop mentioning it in team briefings.'

Rewards

It was agreed early on that no financial rewards would be offered as part of the quality improvement initiative. A suggestion scheme is well established within the company. This remains the focus for financial rewards and continues to be very important for some people. It was thought necessary to create a climate whereby people wanted to participate for the pleasure of being able to change things themselves and for the pride in a problem being well solved. In this case recognition was its own reward. As a result, quality awards are modest and really aimed only at saying a public 'thank you'. These small awards include the following:

- A mug with logo, for everybody joining a quality circle or quality action team – 350 mugs claimed to date.
- A pen and clipboard with logo, once the first project has been completed – 200 pens and clipboards claimed to date.
- A sweatshirt with logo, once four projects have been completed – 40 sweatshirts claimed to date. This award has been found particularly useful in encouraging the step-by-step, project-by-project culture.

However, probably the most important reward is acceptance of the recommendations of project teams. The evidence is that teams are very thorough and sensible, as well as cost conscious when developing their solutions. They can be trusted to solve their own problems and this trust is demonstrated by accepting their solutions. The site director at Cardiff boasts that 'No recommendation from a quality circle or local action team has so far been turned down.'

New skills

The ongoing aim is to continue the training and education of the workforce. The next target is to have experts trained in selected new skills so that when the need arises they can act as tutors to project teams. In this way, advice and training on many topics can be delivered at the appropriate time to meet the teams' needs. This helps to nurture the individual, since some people get a real thrill out of becoming the local expert.

Nearly 20 per cent of the workforce have attended these skill-broadening sessions since they began in 1991.

The aim of the final stage in the training for quality programme was to introduce new tools and techniques into the problem-solving and planning arenas. The initial strategy was to train local experts to champion the new techniques then, step by step, to scale up the training. The process was begun in 1991 by developing three champions who helped project teams when necessary. The base is now being broadened and further in-house courses are being organized for more and more participants.

Learning from success and failure

The relationships between the quality improvement process and the company are outlined in Figure 1.3.

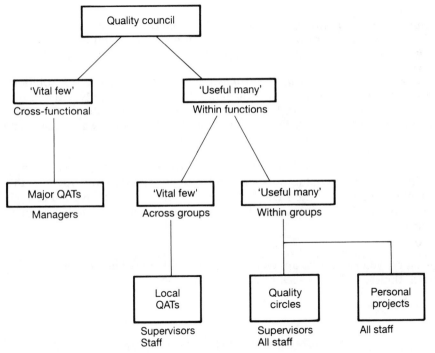

Figure 1.3 The relationships between the quality improvement process and company organization

The sharing of successes and the discussion of difficulties, both when implementing solutions and in the problem-solving process itself, were fostered and encouraged in a number of ways:

- Facilitators met twice a month to discuss problems and how to improve the process continuously.
- Quality circles and quality action teams met quarterly. A value rating of 76 per cent was given during feedback from these trial meetings in 1990. This led to a decision to pioneer the meetings in the major production group in 1991. As

teams became established, these general meetings were phased out. They are now used only when a new technique or approach is being introduced. Subsequent feedback now suggests that the meetings should be extended across the entire site, and many innovative ideas have resulted from them.

- The in-house newsletter, *Quality Circular*, publicized successful solutions, teamwork and new ideas.

Challenges in Phase 3

In addition to having the supportive framework in place, increasing participation, particularly voluntary participation, requires line managers to show that they value their people and their contributions. This behaviour can be a challenge, and experience has indicated some traps to be avoided:

- *Thinking only you can have useful ideas*   Avoid the temptation to keep on stepping in with your own ideas. This is a sure way to inhibit involvement. Prove that you value individual contributions by 'holding your tongue' and listening.

- *Thinking you must solve all the problems*   Do not veto projects or solutions except for exceptional reasons, which need to be very carefully and sympathetically explained. Face up to the fact that teams will not always do things the way you would. Why should they? Doing it their way means that they will buy into the solution.

- *Thinking it does not apply to you*   Do not expect people to behave one way with their problems and not to notice if you fail to do the same with yours. If the problem-solving process is good enough for them, it should be good enough for you. So learn the techniques and then, most of all, set an example by using them.

Remember, you cannot be an agent of change without asking, discussing and doing different things, and being *seen* to do different things.

PHASE 4: BUSINESS ALIGNMENT

The first three phases – providing the vision, management action and increasing participation – helped Cardiff Laboratories to increase participation by letting people choose their own projects. During the evolutionary process it was seen that these efforts required better coordination if they were to be linked and if more focus was to be given to the overall business goals. There was a perceived need to move away from simply 'reducing hassle' and towards emphasizing and eliminating non-value-added work and, in so doing, reducing lead times.

Department purpose analysis, a methodology developed by IBM, benchmarking and ISO 9002 were the means chosen to give greater business alignment in Phase 4.

Department purpose analysis

As some of the established quality circles matured, they looked for more demanding projects, but an adequate process to support this shift in emphasis was not in place. The answer adopted by Cardiff Laboratories was to use departmental purpose analysis. Departments have been able to focus on their business purpose and then systematically to identify non-value-added activities, along with deficiencies in internal customer service levels – hitting where it really hurts.

In practice the quality circle decides the main work to be done by its section and then matches that to the agreed purpose of the section – looking for non-value-adding activities. It advises the customer of the output in order to discover whether it is meeting the customer's expectations.

To date a quarter of the departments and sections have used departmental purpose analysis to generate a list of opportunities for improvement which will be a source of projects for several years. The process has also drawn in newcomers to project work.

The next planned phase is to explore process analysis and management focus on the cross-functional business processes. Involvement here will be required at all levels in a coordinated effort to improve these processes. New and additional training will form the basis of teaching new skills and encouraging involvement.

Benchmarking

To provide a greater challenge when checking on overall progress, a four-pronged approach has been adopted:

- Moving from using the four stages of quality to using Baldridge award criteria for judging progress. A self-assessment approach is currently being developed.
- As well as using award criteria to improve the four stages of quality, the company tested itself by entering the awards themselves. Success in winning a National Training Award in 1991 led the company to enter and subsequently reach the final of the Perkins Award organized in the UK by the National Society for Quality through Teamwork.
- Cardiff Laboratories joined the Department of Trade and Industry's list of companies which seek to host visits from the rest of UK industry. This provided the opportunity of seeing how the company's processes and ideas stood up to the scrutiny of visiting companies.
- External customers are used to pass judgement on quality improvement efforts. The commercial division invited key account customers in the pharmaceutical industry to visit the Cardiff site and judge for themselves the improvements made in caring for their products. A liaison has also been established with local health authorities to share ideas for mutual benefit.

ISO 9002

One of the next goals is to achieve certification to ISO 9002. The final audit has now been completed and recommendation made for certification.

The original intention was to leave ISO 9002 until later. It was planned to continue to improve all aspects of the business until compliance with the standard was eventually achieved. However, in 1992 feedback was being received that some, but by no means all, of the European customer base were asking whether Cardiff Laboratories was certified. A decision was therefore taken to seek early certification.

An audit was undertaken by external consultants, but since many of the systems and much of the documentation were already in place as a result of the quality improvement process, it was estimated that as much as 85 per cent of the work had already been done.

During the evaluation process it was found that the culture of continuous improvement has been a tremendous asset. On site the necessity for systems and documentation was well understood. Several quality circles and quality action teams have proposed standing operating procedures as part of the move to standardize remedies and to hold on to gains already made.

THE SUCCESS STORY SO FAR

It can be very rewarding to see teams working together to solve problems; to see the effective solutions that result; and to see the enthusiasm that can be generated from successes. But how can a value be placed on these? According to Deming, 'The most important figures needed for management of any organization are unknown and unknowable' (1986). Some of the projects have made savings and of course these can be reported, but it is considered that many of the savings may underestimate the real value of participation.

Major projects

The major quality improvement achievements made so far are outlined below:

- The cost of poor quality was reduced by over £3 million for major projects.
- Savings of over £600,000 were made by quality circles and quality action teams.
- Lead times for testing the biggest product range fell by 80 per cent.
- Lead times for preparing one product range fell by 80 per cent.
- Housekeeping standards rose by 60 per cent.
- The reliability of the biggest product range rose by 60 per cent.

Participation

Securing the involvement of individuals is considered by Amersham to be the central theme of quality improvement. The ultimate goal is the elusive one of total participation. Together with continuous improvement, achieved step by step, project by project, this theme has been used to expose more and more of the workforce to an increasing number of projects, with the ultimate aim of total company participation. Participation so far has involved the following:

- There have been over 200 quality circles and quality action team projects.

- 70 per cent of people at Cardiff Laboratories have participated in at least one project (80 per cent in some areas).
- Two of the original four quality circles are still active after three years.

Lessons learned

A chronology showing the progress of the quality improvement process is given in Figure 1.4.

1988
April — Launch of quality improvement.
First quality council.
June — Training for project leaders begins.
August — First 'vital few' projects.
September — Launch of four stages of quality.

1989
January — Launch of manufacturing excellence.
April — Launch of quality policy.
Training for quality circle leaders.
June — Trial quality circles begin.
October — First quality circle project is completed.
November — First Quality Day celebration.

1990
March — Newsletter is launched.
June — Quality awards are introduced.
August — Company reorganization.
Cardiff quality council is launched.
November — First Quality Day exhibition.

1991
June — Facilitator group is introduced.
July — Specialists are nominated to champion SPC, Taguchi methods, FMEA, QFD.
November — National training award is won.
First external guests at annual Quality Day exhibition.

1992
January — SPC training begins.
March — Department purpose analysis training begins.
May — Experimental design user group is formed to promote experimental design and Taguchi methods.
July — Launch of DPA trials.
November — First customer and supplier posters at annual Quality Day.
December — Hosts first visit under DTI 'Inside UK Enterprise' scheme.

1993
February — First in-house training in Taguchi methods.
Benchmarking – first self-assessment.
March — ISO 9002 certificate is presented.

Figure 1.4 The quality improvement process

Achieving a 'world-class standard' was set against the four stages of quality, and a step-by-step, project-by-project approach was adopted to achieve it. The process of achieving best manufacturing practices has been introduced into a number of areas:

- Process documentation.
- Standard operating procedures.
- Raw material supply.
- Inventory control
- Process reliability.
- Packaging materials rationalization.
- Process development.

During the process of introducing these practices, a noticeable change has been seen throughout, but particularly in the culture of the organization. The original company background was one of scientific excellence leading to a research and development culture rather than one committed to excellence in manufacturing. A large proportion of the workforce are young people, recruited directly from further and higher education. There has always been a feeling among this group, primarily because of their lack of experience, that the company was unique, that it used best practices and that there was little that could be learned from other industries. Furthermore, manufacturing has always been seen as a repetitive and uninteresting activity rather than a source of competitive advantage. The setting of new standards of world class based on the practices and achievements of other companies, then working step by step, project by project to make it happen, has slowly changed the thinking and culture at Cardiff Laboratories over the last four years. Cardiff has laid the foundations and is now well equipped to maintain the progress in order to drive forward to meet the goals of manufacturing excellence and world-class quality.

Although a good start has been made to the quality improvement process, there is always a feeling that any organization could have done better. There is still so much more to do. For example, 30 per cent of the workforce at Cardiff have yet to become actively involved. The key lessons learned so far by Amersham can be succinctly summarized as follows:

- *It is hard work*   At all levels and throughout the workforce any quality improvement programme could easily be described as 90 per cent perspiration, 10 per cent inspiration.

- *First things first*   The programme requires considerable structure and organization. Get the supportive infrastructure in place first before anything else is tackled.

- *Everything takes longer than first thought*   Things do not happen overnight and everything invariably takes longer than originally planned for. It takes three or four projects before instinctive quality behaviour is developed.

- *Work with the enthusiasts*   Initially do not try to get everyone involved at once. Remember, step by step, project by project – that way success can breed success. Move forward with the willing, and recruit others through their example.

- *Tell people what to do differently than before*   Quality behaviour is not necessarily instinctive and people need to be taught how to approach a task that they may have been undertaking in one way for several years. Training and education are never ending.

- *Publicize, publicize*   Once you have started, do not stop: it will work wonders eventually. If you are to achieve maximum participation, you need to tell everyone. But remember to ensure 90 per cent substance, 10 per cent slogans.
- *Give a helping hand*   It may be convenient to have one facilitator, but in the longer term do not just rely on one. Provide adequate facilitator support initially, and be prepared to modify the arrangements to include and involve others.
- *Hand over to line managers*   Once facilitators have undertaken their tasks, be prepared to phase them out eventually.
- *Recognize participation and success*   Say 'thank you' as often and as publicly as you can.

THE FUTURE

There is a saying in Japan that one should 'sail the boat by looking at the horizon'. No matter where you are on the four stages of quality, it must be ensured that sight of world-class quality is never lost. In practice this means striving for 100 per cent involvement, and focusing projects more and more on the company business processes and goals.

The initial phases of the quality process were essentially reactive. Cardiff Laboratories started out by reacting to problems within the organization and attempting to solve them. However, the business alignment phase has begun to shift to a more proactive approach. The drive to do this will reduce the cycle times to ensure that the processes and systems deliver more effectively to customers. In addition to benchmarking, the company proposes to look towards business process redevelopment to help achieve this. This will begin at management level but will necessarily cascade down the organization. There will be some overlap with department purpose analysis (DPA), although this is still in its infancy. The pilot groups are the only ones so far to have completed the process, and they will bear the brunt of the immediate efforts to increase participation.

With involvement comes empowerment, and one way of promoting this is to move towards self-management teams. The ultimate aim is to achieve a competitive advantage in the market place, so Amersham will be working more closely with commercial colleagues, sharing product and process knowledge with them, and also gaining from them a greater insight into customers' real needs.

GLOSSARY

Failure mode and effective analysis (FMEA)   A means of speculating about the mode by which a product or process could fail in use and then setting priorities for preventive action. Used in manufacturing when planning how to safeguard key production processes. Of potential use in R & D in designing robust new processes.

Industrial engineering methods (IEM)   The application of method study to work processes. These are more rigorous methods than the classic problem-solving tools and can make analysis more valuable.

Kepner Tregoe   A selection of methods for rationalizing complex or ill-defined business situations. The individual methods are: situational analysis; decision analysis; problem analysis; potential problem analysis.

Quality function deployment (QFD)   A method of translating the voice of the customer into precise design requirements for a new product or service. This can then be further translated into requirements for the component and the production process. Its use is still in its infancy at Cardiff Laboratories, but a major potential use appears to be in the design of new products.

Statistical process control (SPC)   Provides an understanding of variation in all areas of the business. Used by project teams to monitor processes and then to plan and measure improvements. Allows a prediction of the capability of the current and new production processes and a comparison with the specification.

REFERENCES

Deming, W. E. (1986) *Out of the Crisis*, Massachusetts Institute of Technology Centre for Advanced Engineering Study; Cambridge University Press, 1988.
Juran, J. M. (1991) 'Strategies for world class quality', *Quality Progress*, vol. 24, no. 3, p. 81.

TWO

CAMPBELL LEE COMPUTER SERVICES:
Developing and maintaining a total quality work ethos

JOHN SINCLAIR
AND
ALASTAIR ARTHUR

TWO

Campbell Lee Computer Services:
Developing and maintaining a total quality work ethos

INTRODUCTION

This chapter looks at the development of a quality improvement programme which was used to refocus the culture of the company and enhance its competitive success. The mechanisms used to promote total quality and instil it as part of the formal structure of the organization are reviewed, together with how the quality improvement process has been adapted as the management team and employees gained and learned from their experiences of total quality management (TQM).

CAMPBELL LEE COMPUTER SERVICES

Campbell Lee Computer Services Ltd is a privately owned company engaged in software and computer application systems engineering. The company was formed in 1977 and provides computer systems based on IBM computers in response to the specific business requirements of its customers. The company has developed considerable expertise in both packaged software and systems as well as customized systems that include an element of design and development.

Campbell Lee provides full customer support throughout the complete product life-cycle: from concept and consultancy through to implementation, system maintenance and enhancement. Its main market areas are as follows:

- Manufacturing
- Distribution
- Financial services
- Accounting
- Food industry specialization

- Systems integration
- Office systems
- Personnel
- Purchasing
- Inventory control
- Payroll
- Vehicle cost management
- Planned preventive maintenance

In common with other companies in the computing and software industries, the company is faced with an image problem related to the nature of computing and software products. In the past, these have been promoted in such a way that the reality of the system rarely lived up to the promise. Therefore, people and management within organizations may have unrealistic expectations and fears associated with the products and services offered by a company such as Campbell Lee.

Many companies, conversely, now have a more sophisticated understanding and appreciation of computer-based systems and are no longer content with a 'black box' approach to the design and implementation of these systems. Their demands and expectations are now different from what they were in the 1970s and the service given to them needs to reflect this change.

Growth and mission of Campbell Lee

The mission statement of the company was as follows:

We will provide
effective and profitable
business solutions
based on
IBM mid-range equipment

Because of changes in IBM terminology, this later became 'full-range' equipment.

In the 1980s, Campbell Lee went through a period of rapid expansion and growth. This resulted in organizational stress being placed on what had, until then, proved a successful way of organizing and running the business. In 1987 the company had 26 employees and management saw it as small and organic with highly motivated individuals. Because of its size, it had an informal climate and a culture that encouraged individual autonomy and rapid decision making.

With the increasing size of the company (70 employees in 1990) and three sites (Falkirk, its main base, and branch offices in Paisley and Aberdeen) there was a perceived need to develop and maintain the original work ethos of the company. It was felt by the senior management team that a previously clearly defined work ethic was starting to be lost as the number of employees increased. This change in the nature of the company is summarized in Figure 2.1.

Prior to 1992, the company was organized as individual geographical branches at Falkirk, Aberdeen and Paisley. Each branch was the responsibility of a branch manager. The directors of the company operated within a matrix structure (Figure 2.2) with the managing director being the only person with clear lines of responsi-

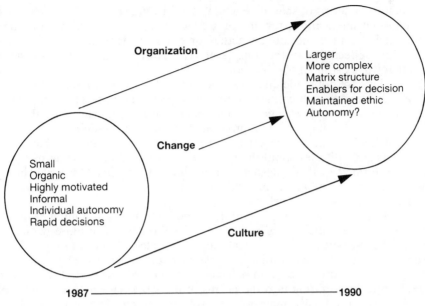

Figure 2.1 The changing nature of Campbell Lee

bility. The other directors had more of a functional responsibility over the wide range of possible company activities.

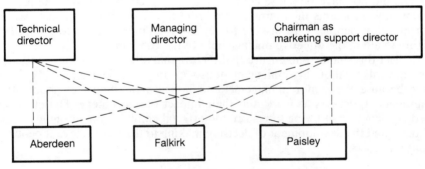

Figure 2.2 Campbell Lee's original structure

Campbell Lee's culture and work ethos

Campbell Lee was founded on technical excellence. This was the driving force in terms of determining the service it offered customers from the beginning of its existence. Since the company started off in a small way, a strong culture of technical excellence was easy to achieve: people were committed to the idea, which provided an initial attraction to work for the company.

Corporate culture is much in vogue, especially with management writers and business consultants, yet it is widely misunderstood. At its simplest, reference tends to be made to culture in terms of shared beliefs, values, attitudes and behaviours. As such, it has important implications for any organization seeking to achieve total quality. However, debates rage on about whether or not management teams can actually change culture effectively in the long term. This is due to the nature of the many cultures that will exist in an organization.

Organizations are not made up of a single culture but exist with many sub-cultures. People may belong to a sub-cultural group whose goals and norms bear no relation to the formal ones espoused by senior management. It is this that can cause the greatest problems for a quality improvement programme in an organization.

Campbell Lee's small size meant that it was in a good position to have a set of shared beliefs and attitudes about the nature of its work and the standards that work should be performed at. Its size also meant that there was no need for a rigid hierarchy and explicit chains of command and communication. Autonomy was encouraged and fostered as a natural way of working.

As the company became larger, and developed into bases at a number of sites, it became much more difficult to sustain this original ethos. With more people in the company, what was successful on a small, intimate scale began to cause problems. As more and more people join a company, they may not be as successfully 'inducted' into the existing overarching beliefs and behaviours of the organization. They may there-fore have difficulty in fitting into the norms of the workplace and the values of the company which in any case may not be explicitly stated. The original values and behaviours of the original members of the company can become weakened as newer members of staff struggle to understand and work in an environment that is alien to them.

With more people at Campbell Lee, new recruits were less aware of the original ethos and did not have the close contact that early recruits had with the founders of the company. Problems in communication and the general management issues of a larger group of people were driving forces in developing a more formalized matrix structure to aid in the effective management of the company.

To reflect this change and ensure that the original ethos was not lost, the company turned towards total quality management as a means of achieving its ends. TQM was chosen because the senior management team saw it as being all about attitudes, commitment, processes at work and their impact on customers. Therefore, it pre-sented an ideal way of trying to restore the original emphasis on autonomy within the workplace and the development of decision making to the most relevant people in the organization.

EARLY DEVELOPMENTS

Management consultants were brought in to undertake a review of the company in 1987. Analysis of this review, conducted during 1988, revealed that the problem was not a management problem or a skill problem, but a *system problem*. It was also realized that quality was much more than BS 5750.

The company, with its concentration of professional, highly qualified staff, is in an unusual situation. Instead of looking towards quality to bring about improvements in productivity and manufacturing/service quality, senior management looked to quality to offset the drift from the original culture of the company, and to equip it to compete effectively in the future.

In drawing up the mission statement, the guiding criterion was that it should be:

Motivating
Informing
Short
Simple
Integrating
Owned and
Needed

The statement was arrived at by the directors and managers with the aid of IBM consultants. To enhance its clarity, the mission statement was expanded to show what it means for everyone at Campbell Lee (Figure 2.3).

MISSION STATEMENT **What does it mean?**	
WE	every person in the company
WILL	commitment
PROVIDE	make available, deliver
EFFECTIVE	producing results
AND	both requirements
PROFITABLE	benefiting all parties
BUSINESS	the community we serve
SOLUTIONS	solve the problem
BASED ON	having strong foundation
IBM	world's most successful IT company
COMPUTERS	the primary ingredient

Figure 2.3   Campbell Lee's mission statement

In seeking help from IBM at Greenock, it became clear that the mechanism to solve the problems being experienced by the company was through quality and, more specifically, total quality management. Management realized that the procedures for building quality into a product or service were essentially similar to those required of a growing business. With growth, there comes a need for more formalized procedures in order to bring about standardized modes of operation and, more importantly, to provide a framework for people to maximize their effectiveness at work. At the same time as bringing about formalization to aid in management and communication within a company, attention has to be given to ensuring that these do not impede job performance by providing a restrictive framework which discourages the use of initiative.

Nineteen eighty-nine was therefore a year of action for the company. It decided to adopt TQM and implement an involvement programme for everyone. One of the project managers took on the role of quality manager and the task of learning about quality. A key point that needs to be emphasized here is that TQM was chosen as an initial path deliberately in preference to the formal quality system that is BS 5750. Initially (in 1988), senior management felt that the standard was too rigid to be of value to the company.

IMPLEMENTATION OF THE QUALITY IMPROVEMENT PROGRAMME

The company attitude to total quality management

TQM for Campbell Lee is made up of a number of key interrelated aspects (Figure 2.4). In particular, it involves three elements:

- Understanding the customers' needs.
- Completely satisfying the customers now.
- Continuously improving the company's ability to satisfy its customers in the future.

The process element of TQM is seen as being much more than a system. It embraces everything that is needed to change the company culture. Campbell Lee has therefore examined its structure, communication channels, methods of management and the general interaction between employees and their customers.

TQM entails an attitude and behaviour change on the part of every employee. This point is made by many people, but is very difficult to accomplish. Some people's level of commitment will be much less than others', and this has to be expected. Such people will require more encouragement and support in coming to terms with changing their attitudes and behaviour. Again, a supportive sub-group culture and overall corporate culture makes it easier to develop a climate where employees are aware of the impact they have on customer relations.

TQM also involves seeing everyone in the company as a 'customer', receiving products or services from colleagues. This is a point that many CEOs and senior managers would do well to remember when quality improvement is being considered. Campbell Lee's senior management were the initiators and initial company 'experts' on quality, cascading this knowledge down through the organization and facilitating total quality in a proactive way.

There is no standard solution involved in TQM, and companies must be wary of trying to apply pre-packaged solutions without any thought being given to the company's own unique context. Staff at Campbell Lee are expected to become aware of and accept the concept of continual, ongoing improvement, and are encouraged to draw up personal quality improvement indicators/plans and to join a quality circle. They also recognize that the customer is the business and that it is important to be courteous to customers at all times. Staff are made aware that company-wide quality improvement involves not doing more work, but doing the same job better: doing the same work, more accurately, more reliably and in a better way, not just once but continuously. This is translated into the aim of providing products and services which do *not* come back, to customers who do.

The quality improvement strategy of Campbell Lee is built into the mission

CASE STUDY 1
QUALITY IMPROVEMENT PLANS

In 1991, the quality improvement plan was included in a business growth training project with Forth Valley Enterprise (a local enterprise company equivalent to the TECs in England). In essence, this plan had the following aims:

- To improve productivity by 6 per cent.
- To reduce the level of rework by 30 per cent.
- To reduce non-customer-related activities by 20 per cent.
- To attain BS 5750 Part 1 quality registration.
- To improve managerial efficiency.
- To improve the profit/turnover ratio by 1.5 per cent.
- To improve internal communications.
- To retain the position of the company as number one in the UK for the IBM customer satisfaction award.

For 1992, the quality improvement plan was more formally stated in the following terms:

- To achieve BS 5750 Part 1 registration before June 1992.
- To monitor business management measurements, to gauge their usefulness and to establish a mechanism for monitoring and action where necessary.
- To establish a clear training policy within the Investors in People framework, to be achieved in 18 months.
- To improve business consciousness throughout the company.
- To increase company awareness of TQM and personal quality measures.
- To maintain an effective quality circle programme.

The quality council is responsible for carrying out the quality improvement plan and creating initiatives for quality improvement. This is done through a combination of company and personal assessment initiatives.

Company indicators/initiatives

- *Quality circles* Developing and maintaining a quality circle programme was seen as an important part of the quality improvement strategy.

- *Quality improvement teams* Where topics require immediate action or specific experience, QITs are formed to report within a specific timescale under specific terms of reference.

- *Publicity and the raising of awareness* An important role of the quality council was raising general awareness of quality within the company. A yearly quality slogan and theme are publicized by the quality council to provide a focus on personally applicable aspects of quality improvement. Special quality notice boards were set up in every company location.

- *BS 5750* This was seen as 'formal quality', resulting in written procedures about what must happen within the company in stated areas and situations.

- *Business management measurements* These were originally stated as cost of quality measures. Graphical information derived from timesheet data completed for work undertaken for customers was published to provide a visible performance indicator and to increase awareness.

CASE STUDY 1 (*continued*)
QUALITY IMPROVEMENT PLANS

Personal indicators/initiatives

- *Quality indicators*   These were split into three categories: (a) company – the provision of some form of measurement by which to assess performance (e.g. by setting a quality theme/slogan); (b) unit – units were allowed to provide their own quality indicators; (c) personal – company personnel were encouraged to set and monitor their own personal quality indicators.

- *Recognition awards*   Individual recognition is given to personnel showing high standards of achievement in meeting both the company quality slogan/theme and receiving unsolicited written testimonials from a customer.

- *Quality induction*   Every person joining the company goes through an induction process based on quality, TQM, BS 5750 and the company.

- *Staff reviews and surveys*   Every member of staff has an annual review with the opportunity to complete a staff survey questionnaire. Results from these are collated, analysed and presented in statistical form for planning purposes, and provide feedback on perceptions of company performance.

Design of programme/process

Campbell Lee's approach to quality initially drew on Crosby's philosophy, making use of the quality triangle of product, process and customer, together with the four absolutes of quality:

- The definition of quality is *conformance to requirements*.
- The system of quality is *prevention*.
- The performance standard is *zero defects*.
- The measurement of quality is *the price of non-conformance*.

This translates into the 3D service quality approach:

- *The product and service dimension*   The degree to which customers are satisfied with products and services.
- *The people dimension*   The degree to which customers are satisfied with the relationship they have with the people at Campbell Lee.
- *The process dimension*   The degree to which the company is satisfied with internal work processes that are used to develop the products and services supplied.

This approach was adopted because senior management believed that a formalized structure was necessary for Campbell Lee to become a 'quality organization'. They also affirmed that everyone should be involved (from top to bottom) and, perhaps most importantly, that quality should be built into the processes in operation and not viewed as something different. Collective responsibility was emphasized from the outset.

---

statement and the associated company goals, which are drawn up in terms of defining success for the company as follows:

100% first option	Be 100% first-choice option in competitive situations.
People	Provide the environment for people to develop their full potential.
Profit	Be profitable to secure the future of the company and its customers.

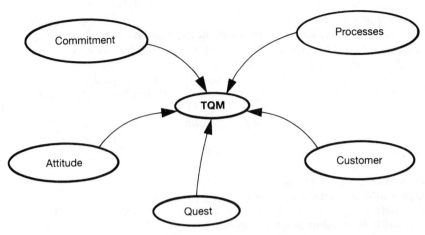

Figure 2.4 Interrelated aspects of TQM

| Quality service | Add value through quality service. |
| Improvement | Make continuous irreversible improvement a way of life (see Case Study 1). |

Management structure

In order to provide an appropriate framework for total quality management, Campbell Lee set up a quality structure, the elements of which are shown in Figure 2.5.

Figure 2.5 The quality organization structure

Steering committee

The roles of the steering committee are as follows:

- To meet quarterly.
- To agree strategy and the approach to quality.

- To coordinate events.
- To agree cost of quality indicators and monitor progress.
- To set quality improvement goals for managers and the company.
- To receive quality circle presentations.
- To discuss quality issues arising from quality circle presentations.
- To support and promote quality consciousness throughout the company.

Quality council

The quality council has the following roles:

- To meet every three weeks.
- To promote understanding of the quality programme.
- To initiate actions to achieve the objectives of the steering committee.
- To provide leadership of quality initiatives.

Quality manager

The roles of the quality manager are as follows:

- To report to the managing director.
- To act as the executive arm of the steering committee.
- To assist in defining policies that will support and develop the quality programme.
- To administer the quality programme.
- To provide training and advice on quality issues.
- To act as facilitator to quality circles.

The quality circle process

Campbell Lee obtained the help of IBM (Greenock) to initiate a circle programme. Circles were seen as comprising a voluntary group of people, usually within a department or branch, who meet regularly on company time to identify, analyse and solve job-related problems in their own area. They were an example of participative management in action, and a means of allowing non-management staff the opportunity to contribute to the creation of a more successful Campbell Lee and a more satisfactory working life.

The circles were piloted at the Falkirk headquarters and then became company-wide, including branch circles, finance/administration and sales and marketing. Training was initially based on IBM quality circle training and involved an introduction to problem-solving and presentation techniques.

Management felt that one of the most significant obstacles to understanding and progress in quality improvement is that much of the quality literature and systems were born of manufacturing industry. Campbell Lee is effectively a 'service' company without a 'product' in the accepted sense of the word. It offers services and software products that are intangible to customers, who may in any case have only vague ideas of their requirements. They also felt that general views of industry at large that quality circles do not work, and certainly not in a software environment, offered little in the way of real external assistance from similar companies.

Campbell Lee saw quality circles as equipped to examine fuzzy, undefined problems. Despite the uncertainties, it was felt that circles were one of the most powerful vehicles for TQM, providing benefits in terms of being able to monitor the organization and offering a focus for staff development in what was a recognized training area for the company.

Members of the quality circle gain experience of putting into action a range of problem-solving techniques and having to prepare reports and recommendations on their findings. Presentations of findings are always made to the steering committee, and it has been found that this is one of the most valuable learning experiences for people. Some members of the circle have never taken part in a formal presentation before, and the chance to take part often leads them to feel more confident in making formal presentations to customers.

One of the main difficulties encountered by quality circles at Campbell Lee was the choice of problems. These tended to be far too large and broad for a quality circle to solve. Some people felt that a long time was spent in trying to find something that could be tackled and solved with some chance of success. These feelings are, in part, related to the business of the organization and its underlying corporate culture.

It was felt that quality circles in a manufacturing setting can expect more success and earlier achievement of solutions. Examples were given of deciding to do something about oil spillages on the floor and untidy work areas. Within a professional environment, scope for such projects are limited or non-existent. The feeling that people are providing a minor solution with no effect on the bottom line can threaten to destroy the potential benefits of working as a group.

These issues were felt to be an experiential problem. Quality circles did not know how to choose simple problems and therefore got bogged down, leading to a lack of motivation. It is important that circles receive guidance and support to ensure that they do not disband in disarray.

The circle programme is really seen by senior management as a form of practical training. People often realize that a problem is not as easily solved as they first believed. This helps them to develop a deeper understanding and appreciation of the factors that impinge on both a problem and its potential solution.

The downside from senior management's point of view comes from the delivery issue. Members of circles often see failure in terms of not having their proposals accepted by the steering committee. In Campbell Lee, stress was therefore laid on finding mechanisms for increasing the understanding of circle members of the processes that lead to decisions being made on projects. This has meant an emphasis on the cost/benefit of the proposals.

Each circle is obliged to document its research, proposals and cost/benefit measurements. These are then presented in much the same way that business solutions are presented to customers. This internal exposure to presentation and documentation skills, including the prioritization of activities, is never seen as failure when things are not implemented. What individuals have achieved is the learning exercise of doing the work and completing the quality circle process. Emphasis is put on applying this learning in circle members' day-to-day work.

Quality improvement teams

The development and use of quality improvement teams (QITs) arose partly out of dissatisfaction with quality circles and the changing needs of the quality improvement programme. QITs were initially used in 1991 as a force for improvement and as a faster way of dealing with problem areas.

The Campbell Lee QIT is appointed for a specific task and given a timescale within which to report. It may be either management- or employee-driven, and a team is made up of members drawn from any appropriate section of the company. The QIT is given authority to use company resources, and is free to express conclusions, make decisions and act. In this way, it is a force for quality improvement.

In late 1990, the company decided that there was a need for a formal quality mechanism under BS 5750 Part 1. This was now felt to be appropriate, the standard having been developed since its first introduction and the preliminary foundations having been laid within the company with regard to quality procedures. Moreover, because of pressures from the competitive environment, and the growth in customers requiring certification, Campbell Lee felt that, without it, the company would be at a competitive disadvantage.

The task facing the company was to document the informal practices that were already in existence and to see if and how these needed to be developed. A decision was made to draft a series of codes of practice for the company which set out formally the procedures in the company and provide the basis of an audit trail through its procedures, processes and documentation. A QIT was formed to undertake this work and the task delegated to an owner and author who between them produced a code of practice for their area. These codes were then ratified by a complete management team and became part of the draft quality system documentation.

In moving towards a more formal system of quality assurance and improvement, the company began to adopt standardized ways of identifying, correcting, measuring and reviewing issues that related to quality (Figure 2.6).

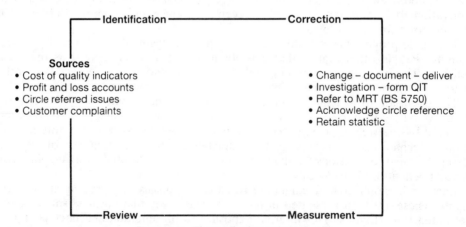

Figure 2.6   The quality improvement cycle

Problem identification started with the use of business process quality management (from IBM). This involves a matrix of processes and critical success factors from which a composite 'weighting' is obtained for each process. From this matrix, action could then be taken in specific areas. The management team was trained in its use and began to adopt it. This was kept separate from the quality circle programme, which was still used to identify and define difficulties and to implement solutions.

During 1991, it was realized that a lot of information from quality circles could be lost because the selection process used was designed to choose one topic from a selection identified by the circle. A 'refer to management' procedure was instigated, where circles preserved their list of problems so that these might be tackled by individual managers or could be used to highlight a common problem for the company. A major finding from this reporting process was that many grass-roots difficulties could be addressed through use of the company codes of practice and procedures.

The use of the matrix gave way to QITs. Management found that the general mechanisms they were using for total quality provided the means to identify and correct problems effectively. They also found that the system was not dynamic enough for their needs. In arriving at a weighted average array of critical success factors and activities, management felt that the problems they were dealing with were too dynamic for the process. The subjective process of weighting, and the speed with which problems change, meant that the system did not provide value on a company-wide basis. It may prove to be of more use at the unit level and this is currently being investigated.

Codes of practice

The development of codes of practice was seen as a way of formalizing good practice and as an appropriate vehicle for education purposes. The aim was to involve as many staff as possible in discovering how things are done within the company and then to document the results. The process promoted the idea of ownership (of issues and problems that affect individuals in their day-to-day work) and served to illustrate the effectiveness of the QIT to a wider audience.

Campbell Lee summarizes the purposes of codes of practice as follows:

- It is necessary to discover how the company operates, and have a common understanding of these procedures. The best way to do this is to document them for all to see.
- These procedures, as codes of practice, then become part of the company quality system, and are required by BS 5750.
- Having documented the codes of practice, there then exists a known baseline from which further developments may take place.

The existing codes of practice are briefly described below.

- *Technical support* This concerns the provision of specialist technical support in IBM systems to complement the company programming and application skills. It includes the support of company computer systems, systems assurance, the dissemination of information regarding technical developments and the provision of technical education.

- *Proposal log* This is about how customer enquiries become firm proposals and are identified and logged. It includes the activities required during the period from enquiry to received order.

- *Order processing* This concerns software and hardware (both IBM and third party), time spent in special projects, and the interface between proposal log, project management and customer education.

- *Customer education and training* This is about how Campbell Lee provides education and training services to customers. It covers enquiries, course programmes, enrolment/booking, course conduct and evaluation, and billing after the event.

- *Replication control*   This is the process by which Campbell Lee ensures that the right version of software gets to the right customer every time. It involves records of what is delivered to customers, software identification, marking, safe storage and controlled modification/upgrading.

- *Software development*   Practices here include file-naming conventions, development standards, utilities and change control. Security and back-up are also covered.

- *Training records and employee induction*   This concerns the procedures which are followed when a new employee joins Campbell Lee, and how employee training records are maintained.

- *Approved suppliers*   The procedure to be followed in purchasing materials and/ or services are contained in this code. It includes how suppliers of goods and services to Campbell Lee are approved for inclusion in the approved suppliers list, and the monitoring of supplier performance.

- *Project management*   This concerns how projects are managed by Campbell Lee, including definition, planning, control and monitoring.

- *Internal audits*   This contains the procedures involved in the auditing of the quality system for BS 5750 purposes, appointment of and training for auditors, planning and scheduling, and auditing records.

Going for BS 5750

In deciding to move towards formal certification for BS 5750, the quality manager, in 1990, felt that for the company to move positively towards this goal required additional internal expertise, especially with regard to formal quality documentation and implementation. This view was accepted and a new quality manager was recruited with appropriate prior experience.

A management review team was set up as a QIT to prepare for certification. The existing codes of practice were used as a basis for the development of an appropriate quality systems manual and related documentation required under BS 5750.

Senior management saw BS 5750 as a quality assurance system very much compatible with total quality within Campbell Lee. In order to prepare effectively for certification, all efforts were focused on documenting and implementing appropriate quality assurance mechanisms within the company. This emphasis led to a drift away from the TQM processes, and it was felt by members of senior management that TQM was put on hold while undertaking the work necessary for BS 5750.

It was generally felt that companies seriously underestimate the amount of work and time required to become BS 5750 certified, and this was certainly the case at Campbell Lee. However, competitive pressures mean that companies like Campbell Lee must seek formal certification whether they feel it is of value or not.

This seeking of formal certification has its roots in the growth of marketing companies on the basis of their apparent 'quality' credentials. There has, over recent years, been a tremendous growth in the number of companies that use BS 5750 as their major marketing tool. There is also the push from customers (both current and potential) for their suppliers to be certified.

Such an overemphasis on this one standard has many dangers. Potential customers may wrongly view a company as providing a quality service or product based on the company's claim that it is certified as a 'quality company' under BSI. Yet this is not really the purpose of a standard which merely confirms that a company has instituted mechanisms and documentation in relation to quality assurance mechanisms. The static nature of the standard could lead to a situation where, once certified, companies move on to their next project while ignoring the need to improve their quality assurance mechanisms continuously. It may also bear no relation to the quality of products and services being offered. The standard is therefore exposed to the risk of becoming devalued owing to lack of regulation on accrediting institutions and the claims made by some certified companies that their products or services on offer are quality ones because of BS 5750.

This is a danger that Campbell Lee's management were fully aware of. In drawing up their documentation, members of the QITs were inclined to seek continually to improve procedures and processes, thus delaying completion of the project. To counteract this, they came to an agreement on reaching targets and then going forward for final certification. Since gaining registration for BS 5750, Campbell Lee has now set up a new QIT to examine its codes of practice and to improve and rationalize them for future use.

Education and training for quality

Campbell Lee's senior management believe that everyone in the company should be aware of the need for quality, and what quality means for Campbell Lee and them as individual employees. The importance of personal ownership was emphasized in the approach adopted to ensure that quality permeates every aspect of the company.

Training for quality is seen as an important way of ensuring that the continuous improvement process has a firm foundation. To aid in this process from the very beginning, every new employee goes through a quality induction programme which introduces him or her to quality and its place at Campbell Lee. The half-day programme covers the essentials of the company's approach, including an overview of how total quality has evolved.

Campbell Lee's company chairman sees one of the fundamental strengths of the company as being the people within it. A high proportion of staff are specialists in their field and arrive at the company with a high degree of education, proficiency and experience. This has led to the company concentrating on training in quality as the major topic for all staff to understand.

At present, there is no formal planning for education and training other than that occasioned by the requirements of the quality programme. This is, however, beginning to change as the company moves on to the next stage of its implementation of total quality and continuous improvement. The main elements of the education and training programme, apart from the induction course for new employees, include the following activities:

BS 5750 roadshow

It was felt that one of the primary requirements for BS 5750 was to inform and educate all staff in relation to the implications and opportunities presented by BS 5750 and the drive towards formal quality within the company. Since misunderstandings and misconceptions existed within the company, the managing director and the quality manager took part in a presentation to all employees, which was repeated in every company location.

Codes of practice

These were used to educate and inform staff of procedures and processes to be applied to key aspects of the company's work. They were also used to demonstrate the effectiveness of a QIT in action.

Auditor training

With the decision made to apply for BS 5750, the company needed internal auditors. A formal training course was developed and held in the company. This was run by the quality manager with the additional use of external quality consultants.

Following on from this training, a total of eight fully trained auditors now exist within the company. They were used in a series of internal audits to monitor the implementation of BS 5750.

Company familiarity

The steering committee recognized that the quality induction programme addressed only part of the company training and familiarity issue. There was also concern expressed that TQM within the company had lost its focus because of a shift towards BS 5750. The committee felt, therefore, that there was a need to redefine the company, its mission, goals and quality objectives, together with individuals' roles and responses to these.

A 'company familiarity' course was designed to help in this process. This was an important consideration because people who have been with a company for some time may often not be fully aware of changes and developments in how quality is expressed and ensured within the company. The course amounted to a retrospective induction programme and took place off site for one and a half days. All personnel have now had the opportunity to learn, question and then understand the company.

Measuring quality

Campbell Lee measures quality in a variety of ways (Figure 2.7).

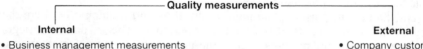

─ Quality measurements ─	
Internal	**External**
• Business management measurements	• Company customer surveys
• Personal quality indicators	• IBM customer surveys
• Customer testimonials	

Figure 2.7   Measuring quality at Campbell Lee

Internal measurements

Business management measurements, which originally started off as cost of quality measures, are statistical graphs derived from timesheet data. This information was used to provide a visible performance indicator and to increase awareness.

It was used, especially initially, to chart rework within the company. Here, rework was seen as remedial work carried out on software systems supplied to customers. In a six-month period, the company saw rework cut in half, but senior management were realistic enough to appreciate that not all of this was due to the quality improvement programme. Some of this decrease was due to a more 'creative approach' to the completion of timesheets.

This can often be a problem in a service-based organization which is dealing with largely intangible products. The management team now believe that the collection of cost of quality data can be counter-productive, and prefer to rely more on seeing quality improvements in action as an indication of how well things are going.

For 1991 and 1992 a quality council decided to adopt measures designed to achieve better *personal quality* focus in the company. A company slogan and theme is chosen for each year. Initially, this concentrated on what quality is:

1989   Quality is in your hands
1990   Quality: take it personally
1991   Quality is 'being counted'

This changed in 1992 because members of the quality council believed they had built up a sufficient understanding within the company about what quality meant. The slogan and theme for 1992 was 'Working to exceed expectations'.

These slogans and themes were designed to help focus everyone's attention on quality being part and parcel of everything that was done within the company. Tangible reminders in the form of pencils, paper-clips and coasters were also used. All personnel were encouraged to design their own personal quality indicators to gauge their performance against the slogan.

Customer testimonials are also used as part of the company's recognition system. Since late 1991, such testimonials have been received steadily and are seen as a reflection of the reality of customer service and quality within the company.

External measurements

In 1991 a *customer satisfaction survey* was undertaken by a QIT. The main customer base was divided between the company's managers, each taking ownership of a group of customers. Questionnaires were then completed during a meeting with customers. After analysing the results, they found that many customers were not aware of the full range of services offered by the company. Some customers aired grievances and each of these was resolved by that customer's 'owner'.

The results of the survey helped to underline what was already felt by the senior management team – that action was needed to provide an increased level of customer care and satisfaction.

The results were also a contributory factor in the decision to restructure the company in 1992 in order to become more customer oriented. The company was reorganized into industry-specific units, which are not necessarily geographically located (Figure 2.8). To facilitate management of the company, clear lines of responsibility were established by allocating directors to individual units.

Each unit is managed by a unit manager and a projects manager. The staff of the units are chosen for their expertise in appropriate areas. Managers are, however, free

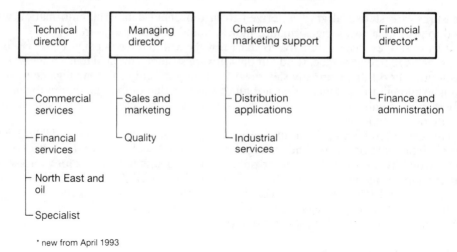

* new from April 1993

Figure 2.8   The post-1992 company structure

to access available staff from other units when necessary. Each of these units has a list of customers with a designated 'customer associate' and salesperson. This has helped to reduce the possible points of contact which customers could have with the company, and has focused on providing a better service to customers.

IBM conducts an annual customer satisfaction survey and ranks its business associates for customer satisfaction. In 1990 Campbell Lee was rated as the number one agent in the UK for customer satisfaction. In 1991 the company went on to miss a customer satisfaction award by less than 1 per cent.

The management team recognize that these are not absolute indicators, but provide clear signs that the company goal of adding value through a quality service is being achieved. Being recognized by an independent survey helped to add weight to this feeling.

Recognition

The company awards 'customer delight' pins for unsolicited letters of satisfaction from customers. These pins have been specially designed for Campbell Lee and are presented to staff at formal sessions during staff meetings. Recipients are not forewarned about the awards. It has been company policy not to become involved in monetary awards, since this can create the wrong climate for promoting continuous improvement for everyone within the organization.

Last year, Campbell Lee used the theme of 'courtesy to colleagues' to help reinforce the importance of viewing people within the company as internal customers. Progress towards achievement of the theme was measured company-wide with branch and unit managers making returns each month, giving the names of staff who had shown an appropriate level of courtesy. World Quality Day was celebrated by a voting process when all company branches voted for the person who had demonstrated the highest level of courtesy. Over 75 per cent of the company took part in the process and 47 per cent of staff members received a vote. Senior management saw this as essentially a light-hearted approach to reinforcing the message that everyone has an impact on the level of service offered within the company and by the company to its customers.

LEARNING FROM EXPERIENCE

Continuous improvement brings with it the need for continuous learning. By learning from activities undertaken to improve quality and by applying this knowledge, a more effective environment is developed where total quality has a greater chance of becoming reality.

Campbell Lee has learnt the following from its experience.

Success needs ownership

For total quality to become reality, an important element is the 'ownership' of the activities that constitute providing a quality service or product. Where people feel involved, participate and are effectively empowered to have a direct impact on what they do in the workplace, they are more likely to take seriously the need for continuous improvement.

Campbell Lee has, through the structuring of its quality improvement programme, given ownership of problems, systems and processes to the very people who have to make them work.

The key driving force is self-esteem

Developing and maintaining a culture which values individuals and their unique contributions makes it easier to achieve the goals of a quality improvement programme. A positive culture which promotes the effect that people have on their day-to-day work, and shows in tangible forms how they can effect change within the workplace, provides the right environment for total quality.

Giving people the confidence to question what they and others do, and providing them with the tools and mechanisms to facilitate changes where quality problems/issues have been highlighted, help to promote individual self-esteem.

The importance of the customer

The place of the customer, both external and internal, cannot be forgotten in any quality improvement programme. Education has a role to play in teaching customers how to specify their needs and requirements more clearly. A better understanding of each other's needs leads to a better partnership and increases the likelihood of delivering what the customer perceives as a quality service.

This question of perception is important and can be overlooked. Therefore, rather than concentrate exclusively on a wide range of quantitatively based quality measures, there is a need to discover what customers' perceptions are and how well services meet these.

Achievement requires teamwork

Achievement of the objectives of Campbell Lee's quality improvement programme required effective teamwork. It is often said that more can be achieved by a team than by an individual, but teams create many problems for organizations. Differing inputs, strengths and weaknesses of individuals within the group and sometimes different objectives mean that teams may not work together as well as they might.

Campbell Lee has seen the benefits of using quality improvement teams to tackle a range of quality-related issues within the company. It has also benefited from seeing individuals' quality circle work translated into their day-to-day activities.

Function replaced by process

Rather than organize in a strictly functional way, Campbell Lee has reorganized to emphasize the processes of the business. This has been done to ensure that customers are better and more effectively served by teams which are organized according to the specialist processes they are involved in.

Understanding comes from involvement

Understanding of the need for change, and bringing it about, come very much from involvement. All levels of staff have been encouraged from the beginning to play an active part in the quality improvement programme. Devolvement of responsibility for quality has helped to ensure involvement across a broad spectrum of the company.

MAINTAINING TOTAL QUALITY WITHIN THE COMPANY

Management at Campbell Lee believe that TQM and quality improvement demand strategy, planning, management and implementation. The company maintains a high-profile involvement by directors and senior managers in quality improvement. They are actively involved in both initiating and maintaining an ethos of total quality in everything that is done within the company.

It was felt that the emphasis on BS 5750, in part, caused a drift away from a total quality approach within the firm and could provide a straitjacket for the company in terms of defining standards, leading people to stick to these and not to view them in the context of continual improvement.

Quality circles within the company have had mixed success. Some of this was due to the complexity of the problems that circles tried to deal with and the design of the initial circle programme being more suited to a manufacturing environment.

Failure is seen in terms of failing to fulfil completely a stated mission within the company. Senior management believes that Campbell Lee has had no absolute disasters and that it learns through experience. Therefore, while the circle programme was suspended owing to the pressures of going for BS 5750 registration, the company is going to persevere in order to find the most appropriate format and process within a quality circle environment to suit the company.

New quality circle programme

A new quality circle programme has been developed, taking account of Campbell Lee's experience of its prior programme and the reorganization of the company into units. The key aspects of this new programme are as follows:

- There is a company unit-based approach, although circles will not be exclusively unit based.
- Flexible meeting times.
- Circles will be facilitated by the quality manager.
- Circles will be 'managed' by a forum of quality circle leaders who can coordinate activities and provide support to quality circle members.
- Shorter feedback and corrective action loops.
- Direct visibility, interaction and reporting between quality circles and company units, e.g. at unit and location meetings.
- An emerging definition of the 'mission' of the quality circles.
- The training programme has been retained, but it has now been formalized across the company as problem solving for quality improvement.

An improved understanding has been achieved of the difference between quality circles and quality improvement teams. This has led to an emphasis on teamwork and the integration of quality circles and improvement teams as complementary aspects of ongoing quality improvement in the company. This programme is currently being initiated by the company.

Dropping the 'M' word

The importance of organizational culture and its effects on employees' attitudes, behaviours, beliefs and values cannot be overemphasized. There is a general confusion about corporate culture within companies and how the existing culture will, to a large extent, determine the readiness and success of any planned programme to bring about total quality. Companies often try to implement TQM within a vacuum, with an overconcentration on quality tools rather than looking to their structure and communication channels and the way people are treated in the workplace.

Campbell Lee could be said to be unusual in terms of choosing a total quality path to reaffirm the important elements of its culture and to stop a drift away from its original work ethos. It has built its quality improvement programme with this aim in mind.

The company developed a quality foundation which reaffirmed and emphasized its culture of autonomy and devolvement of decision making. Once this was established, the other aspects of its programme were slotted into place (Figure 2.9). These interrelate and help to reinforce the importance of quality while clearly specifying what 'quality' means for the company. BS 5750 has been used as a small part of this process, to formalize existing good practice.

The company has not made the mistake of seeing BS 5750 as something which gives an organization a quality product or service: companies are free to set their own quality standards. BS 5750 systems merely confirm whether or not the company is meeting these. This can deflect attention away from considering the structural issues within an organization that may inhibit a quality improvement programme, where the

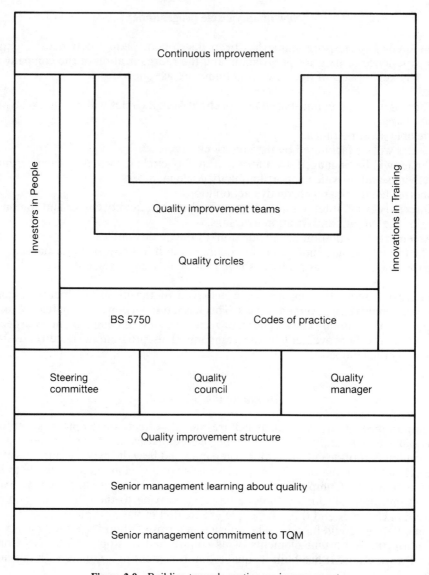

Figure 2.9 Building towards continuous improvement

goal is to create a climate where employees wish to change their attitudes and behaviours in the direction of achieving continuous improvement.

Senior management also believe it is important to minimize or ignore the 'management' in TQM. An emphasis on the management aspect can signal to employees that it has nothing to do with them. Management is implicit in the activities involved in total quality – but it is in terms of managing oneself in identifying areas of individual and group performance which inhibit the delivery of a quality product or service, and being facilitated to take action to rectify the situation. It is also very much about becoming proactive and adopting a longer-term focus, starting to identify potential problem areas or issues that quality improvement teams can tackle, and thus continuously improving the ability to satisfy customer needs in the future.

The basic work approach within Campbell Lee is based on the belief that the company can make its systems do almost anything, but that only the customers know what they need. However, customers often need to be helped to achieve a clear understanding of their own needs and the ability to express these needs in a way that leads to the development of a 'product' that satisfies them. Campbell Lee used total quality as a way of helping this process of better satisfying its customers.

Total quality is seen as an exciting venture by the company chairman. He believes that, with the introduction of such vehicles as quality circles and quality improvement teams, the workforce are resolving their own problems and that the company is in a 'no lose' situation.

Total quality was identified as an empowerment tool. The growth of the company and its drift away from an original culture which stressed autonomy meant that newer employees expected 'management' to make all the decisions and to delegate to them as appropriate. This attitude was felt to stifle the dynamic atmosphere within the company, and to lead to the bottom of the company's vertical structure becoming less effective.

The company having adopted a total quality approach, the chairman believes that people at the bottom of the structure have become re-empowered. They were asked to become involved and to document what they did and how they dealt with the issues of their day-to-day work. The new approach also helped to change senior management consciousness of the problem. The formalization of quality, with its emphasis on circles and the measurement of effectiveness in terms of costs and benefits, offered the company clear guidance on its requirements, but for Campbell Lee this was not as significant as the re-empowerment that took place within the company.

Management commitment has been evident from the start at Campbell Lee with the impetus coming from senior management. They have become fully involved in total quality activities which they do not delegate. They are also involved at all levels within the organization. Involvement is the key word as far as they are concerned. Total quality is fundamental to the business and is treated as such.

The major benefits

A number of major benefits have arisen from adopting a total quality approach at Campbell Lee:

- It has helped to clarify what had amounted to a problem of the 'ethic' within the company. This led to a re-evaluation of the way the company went about its business and the role of everyone within it.
- By adopting a reflective approach to the processes within the company and how it was organized, the company restructured in order to facilitate the re-empowerment of the workforce and to encourage everyone to see that they can have a direct impact on what they do and can bring about effective change.
- This has led to a greater understanding of the role of the formalized structure that was introduced, and how it is designed to support and help people in their day-to-day activities. The expectation on the part of some people that the structure was there to act as a delegation mechanism has been removed. Instead,

senior management have used total quality as a tool to devolve aspects of management to everyone in the company.

- This structural mechanism provided the foundation for the development of processes and practices that were used to address BS 5750. Delivery of the necessary quality system could not have been achieved without the benefit of the company's total quality approach.
- People were actively involved in the formal documentation of work standards and processes which they owned.

The commitment issue

There is general agreement among writers and consultants about the need for commitment from everyone in an organization. Yet this is going to be difficult to achieve for many reasons. Not everyone sees the same need for change, or the personal benefits that they will gain from giving their commitment to any proposal for change.

Campbell Lee has a heavy concentration of highly educated individuals who might be thought likely to want to be involved and to be committed to what is being done. But with any kind of change, there are likely to be those who are less enthusiastic or perhaps hostile to proposed changes.

The company chairman at Campbell Lee does not believe that everyone needs to be committed to total quality. However, he sees commitment as a measure of success, where those who are not committed feel left out of things. People who have negative views on continuous improvement are often given something to do in the programme. They are then in a better position to build an understanding of what the company is trying to achieve and at the same time are given the opportunity to show why they believe things will not work. They are given the opportunity to try to influence others concerning the relevance of their viewpoint and to justify their stance in relation to quality improvement proposals. Quality improvement teams have been seen to be a particularly effective tool in regard to this. Non-committed people are allocated to a QIT and given the opportunity of seeing that they can change things. For Campbell Lee, this approach is considered to have been successful.

THE FUTURE

Senior management at Campbell Lee are committed to the philosophy of continuous improvement and see this as the way to keep the company at the leading edge in the provision of services to its customers. They also realize that, by committing themselves to continuous improvement, they are calling for an ongoing investment in the development of the workforce.

The future strategy of the company with regard to equipping people to improve continuously what they do is to invest in training and development activities for everyone in the company. The most appropriate vehicle for this is seen to be the Investors in People scheme. The company has already registered its intent to seek certification under the scheme and hopes to achieve this in the next year or so. It is also investigating the TickIT scheme launched by the Department of Trade and Industry, which relates specifically to the quality of software products.

Linked to the development of activities to become Investors in People, the company is taking part in an Innovations in Training initiative in conjunction with the local enterprise company. To this end, it is developing multimedia-based training packages for its staff.

By clearly investing in the training and development of its staff in order to improve their abilities to meet customer needs both now and in the future, Campbell Lee believes it has regained its original work ethos, which placed emphasis on the empowerment of people to achieve the company's mission.

REFERENCE

Crosby, P. B. (1979) *Quality Is Free: The Art of Making Quality Certain*, McGraw-Hill, New York.

THREE

HYDRAPOWER DYNAMICS:
Service delivery improvement in a small organization

STAN ZETIE
JOHN SPARROW
ALAN WOODFIELD
AND
TOM KILMARTIN

THREE

Hydrapower Dynamics:
Service delivery in a small organization

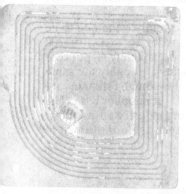

INTRODUCTION

Hydrapower Dynamics Ltd is a small Birmingham-based company of 25 people engaged in the assembly and sale of hydraulic hose assemblies. This chapter describes their progress towards total quality and, in doing so, focuses on two aspects:

- Implementing total quality in a small organization.
- Customer-centred total quality.

Though the latter topic has been written about extensively, we have come across very few references to small organizations in the literature.

The first part of this chapter describes the hydraulic hose assembly market and identifies Hydrapower's niche within it. The second section reviews and discusses the way in which the company has implemented total quality management (TQM), while the third identifies the improvements that have resulted. The fourth section analyses how Hydrapower has succeeded in achieving total quality. The final section attempts to draw general conclusions applicable to small organizations, particularly those in a similar situation to Hydrapower. A preliminary model is formulated which the authors suggest is of value in understanding why some organizations adopt TQM and why others do not.

HYDRAPOWER DYNAMICS

The market place

A hydraulic hose assembly comprises a length of flexible hose, usually of some type of synthetic rubber, with a metal fitting at either end. The purpose of the assembly is to transfer fluid from one point on a piece of machinery to another. The fluids themselves range from passive ones, such as water, through to highly active ones, such as acids. The range of applications is equally widespread. A key user is the construction equipment industry. Hydraulic hose assemblies are used on such things as mechanical diggers, dumper trucks, refuse disposal equipment and fork-lift trucks. Other users include the defence industry, in applications such as torpedo equipment and aircraft refuelling lines, and the commercial vehicle industry.

In addition to complete assemblies there is a demand for loose components, for customers to assemble themselves, and for on-site refurbishment. Hydrapower operates in all three sectors. It also factors a range of 'swaging' machines, which it supplies to customers in the self-assembly market.

The total UK market, excluding the swaging machines, is currently estimated to be worth £200 to £300 million per annum. There are thought to be in excess of 200 suppliers, of whom four or five dominate. They account for approximately 40 per cent of the market. The balance is split between about 50 companies of roughly the same size as Hydrapower and 150 that are even smaller. That only these rough estimates are readily available is an indication in itself of the diffuse nature of the supplier base. The widespread use of hydraulic hose assemblies in the engineering industry ensures that the customer base is equally disparate – ranging from giants such as Ford through to one-person backstreet operations.

Market strategies

Not surprisingly, given this background, the market is highly competitive. It is instructive to analyse it in terms of Porter's five forces model (Porter, 1985) (see Figure 3.1).

The salient features of Porter's model and their interpretation in this context are as follows:

- *Bargaining power of suppliers* – large. The components that make up the assembly, the hose and the fittings, are standard products. Suppliers are not dedicated to this particular market and thus cannot be held to ransom. Should they lose hydraulic hose business, they have other outlets which will compensate.

- *Bargaining power of customers* – large. There are a large number of assemblers all offering technically similar products. Further, the nature of the product is such that it is doubtful that any supplier could establish a technical lead. To the customers hose assemblies are a commodity like sheet steel and nuts and bolts.

- *Threat of new entrants* – large. The assembly process is simple and well known, and the capital required small. This lack of entry barriers could well account for the large number of firms in the market place.

- *Threat of substitute products* – none seen at present. This reinforces the previous point about the large number of firms, in that a technologically stable market is more attractive to newcomers than a rapidly changing one.

- *Rivalry among existing firms* – strong. It is relatively easy for a newcomer to enter the market and take some of an existing supplier's business.

Although they are based on the hydraulic hose assembly market, it is worth noting that these findings apply equally, if not more so, to many of the markets that appear

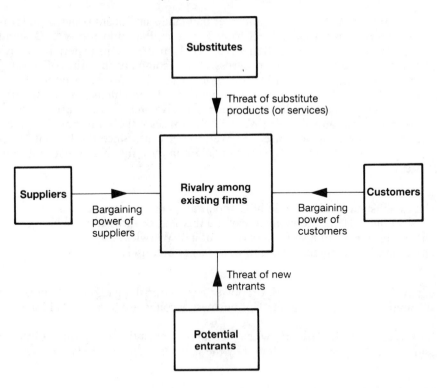

Source: Adapted from Porter (1985).

Figure 3.1 Porter's five forces

attractive to people starting up their own businesses. Two examples are garment manufacturing, where the bargaining powers of both suppliers and customers are even greater than in the hydraulic hose assembly market, and the jobbing building industry.

Of the two generic growth strategies generally considered available to any organiz- ation – cost leadership and product differentiation – the latter is the more appropriate in the environment just described. An attempt to gain market share through cutting costs will only be successful, if at all, in the short term – and at the expense of profitability. Inevitably, given the intense rivalry already noted, a cost cutter would soon find itself, in turn, undercut. On the other hand, there are a number of ways in which a company can differentiate itself from its competitors and generate a more sustainable advantage. Examples include technology, availability, design and packag- ing. The route Hydrapower has chosen to follow is that of *differentiation through quality.*

The company

Hydrapower Dynamics Ltd was founded in 1983. The present company is the result of a management buyout by the present board. The motivation was to avoid a threatened merger by the business's then owners with a bigger company in the same market. Fifty-one per cent of the company was acquired in December 1988; the balance in

June 1989. Prior to the buyout Hydrapower had made significant progress in terms of quality assurance, having gained BS 5750 Part 2 in 1987 and the NATO standard Allied Quality Assurance Publication 4 (AQAP 4) in 1988. This experience provided the platform for the post-buyout progress of the company in terms of developing TQM. It is worth noting here (and this point will be returned to later) that such buyouts frequently act as catalytic events which facilitate changes in the mindset of senior management, often leading to a comprehensive analysis of future direction.

At the time of the buyout there were 13 employees – there are now 25. Over the same period turnover has increased by over 50 per cent. Since the buyout the company has undertaken a number of commercial initiatives, the three most significant of which are as follows:

- The establishment of a mobile hose repair and maintenance service, 'Hosemobile'. There are plans to expand this service through franchising.
- The establishment of a subsidiary operation in Warwick.
- The expansion, early in 1993, into new, larger premises.

Unusually for a firm of its size, Hydrapower has a flourishing export business in third world countries such as Sri Lanka. This business accounts for some 10 to 12 per cent of turnover.

This success story, particularly when measured against the background of the worst recession since the 1930s, is attributed by the managing director to two causes:

- The existence of a formal structure.
- The emphasis on customer-orientated quality.

Both elements are important. While the formal structure, related to the earlier implementation of BS 5750, has obviously played a part, both in terms of the ongoing business and in easing the transition to TQM, it is our contention that the quality dimension is far more significant. There may also be synergy. A formal structure, without any accompanying quality-driven emphasis on customer satisfaction, can lead to rigidity, loss of 'touch' and, eventually, declining market share and profit. IBM can be cited as an example of an organization that was in this situation. Customer awareness was, until the recent market-orientated reorganization, conspicuous by its absence.

The implementation of a quality assurance programme such as BS 5750 is not, however, an essential prerequisite to the adoption of a TQM programme. Though this is the 'standard' textbook approach, we have personal knowledge of a company which has reversed the sequence. This company is currently implementing BS 5750 on the back of a successful TQM programme. It is unlikely that the company is unique.

Supporting evidence for the importance of customer orientation comes from a recent survey of TQM practice in the UK (Whyte and Witcher, 1992). Of those firms in the survey which measured the cost of not meeting quality standards, 80 per cent estimated this factor as being worth up to 20 per cent of their turnover. Whyte and Witcher state: 'We believe TQM ideally starts with the external customer – and if it does not the customer quickly becomes the focus of the TQM effect. Only then does TQM provide real total customer satisfaction.'

THE QUALITY IMPROVEMENT PROGRAMME

Training

The company's initial introduction to total quality came soon after the buyout. The managing and sales directors attending a TQM awareness seminar at a local college. This was followed, in September 1990, by an internal awareness seminar which took the form of an offsite presentation to the staff and the company's major suppliers and customers. Presentations were given by a representative of what was then called the National Society for Quality Circles (NSQC) as well as by Hydrapower management.

The reasoning behind including suppliers was that, if they could be persuaded to join in the initiative, Hydrapower would be able to eliminate goods-inwards inspection. This has not turned out to be the case. Although supplier quality has improved, it has not yet been possible to abolish inward inspection; suppliers do not consider Hydrapower a sufficiently important customer to merit special quality treatment – a good example of Porter's bargaining power of suppliers discussed earlier, and one frequently found in smaller companies. Only now is this supplier attitude beginning to change as a result of the company, as part of its ongoing continuous improvement campaign, working with them to find ways of reducing the supplier reject level.

Other formal external training and education initiatives that the company has undertaken include the following:

- Attendance by senior managers on a management change course.
- A visit by all employees to a large, local Japanese-owned company to study its methods and perceptions of TQM.
- The employment of a consultant from Birmingham Polytechnic (now the University of Central England in Birmingham) to assist in setting up the quality circles programme. This consultancy was funded by a grant from the City of Birmingham's Economic Development Department (EDD).

In addition to these formal commitments there has been a considerable amount of informal, on-the-job training. As Brown (1992) notes, TQM requires training in all aspects of job competences as well as in specific TQM techniques.

In the spirit of continuous improvement there are plans for further training. It is intended, providing that funding is made available by the EDD, to train all employees to a standard enabling them to obtain a recognized quality qualification.

Early developments

An outcome of the initial awareness meeting was that the company set up a quality circle comprising almost the whole workforce. In doing so, they were following the NSQC guidelines which suggested that a circle should comprise 10 to 12 people. While successful, the circle caused problems. In particular, it was extremely disruptive and, more importantly, as a consequence customer service could have suffered. Large organizations, such as those examined elsewhere in this book, also have problems in this respect. The degree of disruption that they suffer is, however, much smaller and relatively easily absorbed.

The TQM process might have stopped dead at this stage, or at least progressed far more slowly than it has, had the company not come up with the concept of *quality bubbles*. A quality bubble is essentially a small quality circle comprising two, three or four people as appropriate. The concept is illustrated in Figure 3.2 (diagram courtesy of Hydrapower Dynamics Ltd).

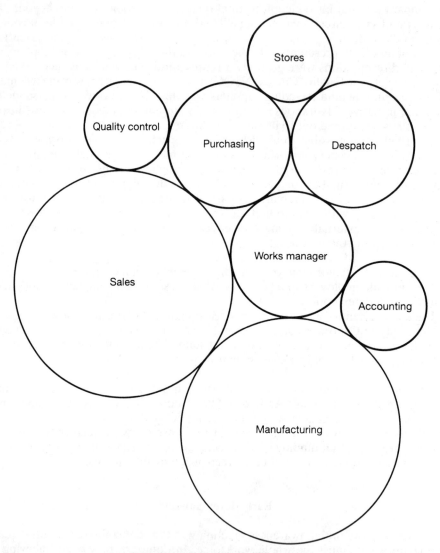

Figure 3.2   The quality bubble concept

The underlying idea is that each department has its own bubble which tackles problems internal to that department. Should a problem cross departmental bound-aries then two, or more, bubbles merge into a bigger bubble. A merging of all the bubbles brings the company back to the original quality circle concept. As well as differing from quality circles in size terms, bubbles also differ in degree of formality.

The formal recording of decisions and the subsequent formal evaluation of ideas, two features of 'conventional' circles, have been dropped. If a proposal put forward by a bubble is self-evidently 'a good thing', Hydrapower will go ahead and implement it; the company has neither the time nor the resources to carry out detailed costings.

This is a higher-risk strategy than that inherent in the more 'standard' quality circle approach. There is a danger that the organization will satisfice rather than optimize and may even, on occasions, take what later turns out to be a wrong decision. Such risk taking is, though, not incompatible with the whole ethos of a small organization. Balanced against the risk is the potential for a more genuine closeness and sharing when discussing ideas and developing a real commitment to change. Again, these factors are more likely to be found in a small organization.

Like their namesakes, the bubbles are ephemeral. There is a danger, particularly in large organizations, of quality circles becoming institutionalized and focused on solving problems for their own sake rather than as a means of improving customer service. This does not happen with Hydrapower's bubbles. They form, perform, dissolve and, when necessary, re-form but perhaps with different members and for a different purpose.

The bubble concept is just one example of Hydrapower making up the rules as it went along. It also reflects the company's intuitive belief in the need to involve the whole organization. It had tried to do this with the original quality circle, but had failed for the reasons already noted. Given the dearth of TQM guidance in the small company area, intuition was, perhaps, the only route forward. To quote the managing director: 'None of the literature we read or the films we watched or the consultants we spoke to had any reference or experience of a small to medium size company trying to implement a TQM initiative. We became pioneers.'

Further developments

In addition to adapting the original scheme by introducing the bubble concept, three further developments have been introduced: flash meetings, a suggestion box and action teams.

Flash meetings are, as the name implies, short, spontaneous meetings of two, three or four people. These can be called at any time and by anyone in response to, and as a forum for solving, a problem which has just arisen. The difference the company sees between these meetings and bubbles is that the latter are directed towards potential rather than actual problems. The distinction, though, is not that clear-cut. The two terms now appear to be used interchangeably within the organization. Both terms, however, reflect a genuine intention to tackle problems through collective effort, whether they are ones that have already materialized or ones that are about to materialize.

An indicator of the informal nature of flash meetings is that no records are kept of how many, or how often, meetings are held. Again, the focus is action orientated rather than bureaucratic. The formalization issue is interesting in this context. In seeking to foster genuine team spirit, there is some reduction in personal control when required, for example, to produce minutes. The team feel that they have learned and that this is sufficient. This may be particularly true of smaller organizations, which often flourish through the rich communication which comes from people knowing and remembering issues rather than through institutionalized procedures. Again, the balance between informality and structure seems important.

The *suggestion box* was introduced as the outcome of a quality circle discussion. It is opened every two weeks and a £15 award made for each accepted suggestion. In addition, there is a £50 award for the best suggestion each quarter and a £500 annual award for the best suggestion each year. It might be thought that a scheme such as this would run counter to the sharing culture of bubbles and circles, in that employees might hold back their ideas for the suggestion box and, hence, financial gain. Experience shows this not to be the case. The ethos of the bubble and circle meetings is such that employees gain greater satisfaction from the shared approval that putting forward an idea in these forums generates than from the essentially personal monetary gain that the suggestion box provides.

Action teams may be formed to tackle specific problems that emerge from bubbles, circles or the suggestion box. Like the other components of Hydrapower's quality structure, they are temporary organizations. Some action teams have only a short life; others, looking at longer-term problems, are less transient. An example of the latter is the action team looking at purchasing procedures. Implementation of this team's proposals took longer than originally anticipated as there were delays in arranging the necessary amendments to the computer system. To speed decision making, action teams always include at least one representative of senior management.

The original quality circle still meets. It is now, though, more of a communications meeting, an opportunity for the whole organization to get together, than a problem-solving forum. It would seem that having created its dynamic offspring, bubbles, flash meetings, action teams and suggestion box, the quality circle itself has become institutionalized. This is no bad thing as it helps to stabilize and formalize the quality improvement process.

The current structure

In formal terms the company sees its quality structure as depicted in Figure 3.3(a). This served as a useful model in the early days of the process, particularly in the sense of showing ongoing quality improvement growing from the BS 5750 quality assurance base via the training and development programme, and in terms of selling the original proposals. It no longer effectively models the present system. Neither bubbles nor flash meetings feature in it, and the implication is that actions result only from the action teams – which is clearly not the case.

The present structure is much more organic (witness, for example, the interchangeability of bubbles and flash meetings already noted) and much more adaptable than Figure 3.3(a) implies. Figure 3.3(b) is an attempt to portray the system as it now stands. Even this modified version suffers from the danger of emphasizing the components of the system at the expense of its holism.

The next stages

In line with the continuous improvement spirit of TQM, Hydrapower has not stopped evolving. There are two main developments currently in process: the introduction of a staff appraisal scheme and a customer care survey.

In many cases, staff appraisal schemes are implemented by organizations as a controlling and, in extreme instances, a disciplinary mechanism. The thinking behind Hydrapower's scheme is the exact opposite. It is aimed at encouraging participation

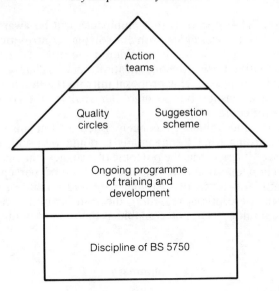

(a) The formal structure

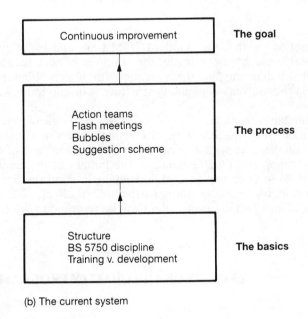

(b) The current system

Figure 3.3   The quality structure

and idea generation. The concept is that employees will be awarded points for any aspect of their work – for example, problem solving, contributing at a meeting or completing a training course – that is considered meritorious. It is also planned to award points for activities outside the organization, such as charity work. These points will be exchangeable for goods. This proposal mirrors the individual financial incentive provided by the suggestion box scheme, but obviates the counter-team-working attitude that the latter could generate.

The customer care questionnaire has been issued as a means of getting feedback from customers regarding what the company is doing well and, more importantly, where it can improve. Its issue was the outcome of a suggestion made by an employee. The brief four-section questionnaire explores customers' perceptions of the company's overall attitude in terms of customer care and quality of service and, more specifically, explores perceptions regarding the trade counter and the Hosemobile repair service. The findings were not available at the time of writing.

Summary

The above description of the quality improvement programme has focused on its structural aspects. There are two reasons for this:

- It is these aspects that make Hydrapower unique.
- These are the aspects that Hydrapower management regard as important.

This is not to say that the standard TQM tools and techniques have been ignored. Considerable use has been made, for example, of such techniques as brainstorming and Ishikawa diagrams, but these are seen simply as problem-solving tools rather than as ends in themselves. The quality structure is orientated towards results rather than technique.

For similar reasons there is no focus on the work of one or more gurus. Some organizations bear the hallmark of Deming, others of Crosby, yet others of Juran. This is not the case with Hydrapower. Although aware of the work of the gurus (witness management's attendance at the initial quality seminar), the company has chosen to go its own way and, while keeping in mind the overall TQM concept, has developed its own implementation structure. In effect, Hydrapower has learnt as it has gone along. This important point will be returned to later.

EFFECTS OF THE QUALITY PROGRAMME

In addition to the overall bottom-line improvements noted at the start of this chapter, the quality programme has led to considerable improvements at the day-to-day operational level. These fall into two classes: one-off improvements and continuous, long-term improvements.

One-off improvements

Improvements of a one-off nature, in the sense that they have had a sudden, dramatic effect, include the following:

- The modernization of the telephone system – in addition to the physical changes to the equipment, the reception and enquiry staff were sent on a telephone answering skills course.
- The investment in a networked computer system – initially to help sales staff improve their response to customer enquiries.
- The redecoration and refurbishment of the retail counter area.
- The adoption of a company logo – the result of a design competition among the employees – which production and counter staff wear on their work clothes.
- The repainting by employees of the workshop – in colours they chose themselves.
- The provision of new work-benches to designs specified by the employees using them.

The two themes common to these improvements are the focus on those aspects of the business that directly affect the customer's perception of the organization, and the extent to which employees have been involved in the decision-making process. Empowerment can be said to be firmly embedded.

In addition to these changes, there have been a number of others introduced in the process of improving the long-term quality measurements discussed in the following section.

Long-term improvements

The company uses three measures to assess its performance improvement over time:

- Number of rejection notes raised on suppliers.
- Percentage of output returned by customers.
- Percentage of orders delivered late.

Figure 3.4 shows the number of non-conforming batches received from suppliers in the period October 1989 to September 1992. Limitations in the current computer systems prevent a finer analysis being carried out, and the company does not consider it worthwhile diverting staff from their customer focus to carry out a more detailed analysis by hand.

Apart from the (perhaps) abnormally low figure for the period from April to September 1990, the figures show a steady downward improvement. The improvement in percentage terms is larger than that shown on the graph as the data are analysed against a background of increasing purchases. The improvements can all be linked to specific actions taken by the company. Examples of such actions include: revising the approved supplier list (effective in the period to September 1990); regrading poor-quality suppliers to a lower grade (period to September 1991); strongly complaining to poor-quality suppliers about the quality of their product (period to March 1992); and retraining inspectors (period to September 1992). These specific

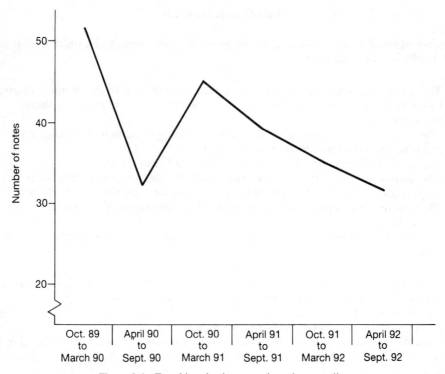

Figure 3.4   Trend in rejection notes issued on suppliers

actions are only part of the picture, however, in that the overall increasing awareness and adaptation of quality concepts – particularly, albeit slowly, by suppliers – will have made a significant contribution.

Figure 3.5 shows, for the same period and for the same level of aggregation, the percentage of output returned by customers for whatever reason. Again the trend line is moving in a downward direction – there is no apparent reason for the 'blip' in the period up to September 1992. This improvement too can be attributed to a combination of specific actions and generally increasing quality awareness.

The specific actions include: having drawings checked by two different people (effective in the period to September 1990); double inspection of finished assemblies (period to March 1991); the introduction of a new method of indelibly stamping information on assemblies (period to September 1991); the purchase of a new swaging machine (period to March 1992); and the provision of new work-benches and tools (period to March 1992).

The final measure, shown as Figure 3.6, is the percentage of orders delivered late on a monthly basis for the period August 1991 to November 1993. In a perfect world there would be zero late deliveries, but it would be unrealistic to expect Hydrapower to achieve this goal on anything except the rarest of occasions – January 1993 with a figure of 1.3 per cent is the closest it has come to date. It should be appreciated that, while a zero target is feasible in an organization that dominates the market it supplies – and thus can control delivery dates – such a target is much more difficult to achieve in what is essentially a jobbing market.

In the absence of significant price competition, the two indicators illustrated in

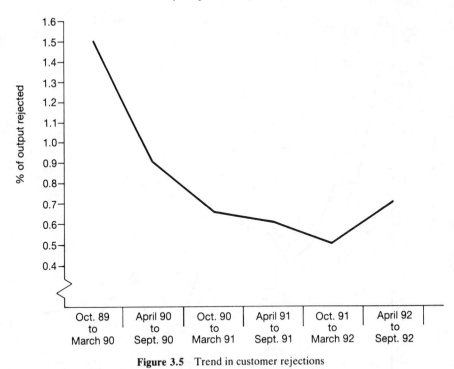

Figure 3.5 Trend in customer rejections

Figures 3.5 and 3.6 are very significant in terms of attracting and retaining business. They are what Hill (1985) refers to as order-winning criteria – the factors that give an organization its competitive edge. The role of modern purchasing management is to minimize the purchaser's total costs rather than the price paid. Both the reduced need for customers to return goods and on-time delivery reduce the costs to the purchasing organization, and hence make Hydrapower a more attractive source than a supplier which does not perform as well against these criteria.

ANALYSIS

The picture that has been painted so far is of a typical small organization, but one which differs in one major respect from the majority of other companies of similar size operating in similar markets. This major difference is that Hydrapower has an explicit, implemented quality mission. Management chose, right from the company's early days, to adopt a quality differentiation strategy and they have followed it through successfully. It is interesting to examine what triggered them to adopt this strategy in the first place and what factors either originally present in the environment or generated from the initial start-up drove the strategy ahead. In examining these questions it is important to appreciate the two major differences between quality assurance and TQM.

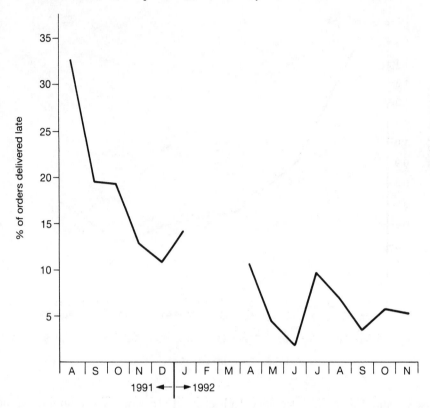

Figure 3.6   Trend in late deliveries

Quality assurance and TQM

The first major difference is that a quality assurance programme is often simply a bureaucratic exercise – a set of procedures that can be implemented mechanically. It need not fundamentally affect the organization's philosophy. Changing the latter, however, is the very essence of TQM. The second major difference is that quality assurance programmes tend to be efficiency rather than effectiveness orientated. As such they focus on the input side of the process rather than the output.

Implementing a quality assurance programme, while time-consuming, is not, in principle, any different from the kinds of change that any organization's management is introducing every day. It is essentially routine. There is little perceived risk. TQM, by contrast, is much more a leap in the dark. The impact of a quality assurance programme can be fairly well predicted; that of a TQM programme cannot be.

Generally, therefore, organizations tend to be much more cautious before embarking on TQM programmes. They need to be strongly motivated, and there is much more inertia to be overcome. Evidence for this statement is given by the numerous references in the literature to companies adopting TQM in response to a crisis situation. The lower-risk, conventional strategies had failed and so they decided to give TQM a chance. A last fling, so to speak. Whether these companies would have adopted TQM irrespective, maybe at some later date, is an open question. It is worthwhile noting in passing that many companies do not proceed beyond the quality assurance stage. It can be argued that this has made them, in their terms, sufficiently successful, and that they see no need to adopt high-risk strategies in the quality area.

The start-up

Prior to the 1989 management buyout, Hydrapower had followed the 'conventional' quality route. Quality assurance standards, both BS 5750 Part 2 and AQAP 4, were in operation – evidence of a management that had recognized the importance of quality. Perhaps nothing more would have happened had not the management team been 'forced' into the buyout situation. This was Hydrapower's equivalent of a crisis. The buyout was a very high-risk, irreversible decision implying a much higher degree of personal financial commitment than before by the then management team. The large number of small organizations, many in a similar position to Hydrapower, that failed in the early 1990s provides adequate testimony for this statement. Given that the buyout decision had already been taken, it can be argued that the proportionate increase in risk that embarking on a TQM programme entailed was relatively minor.

There are other factors operating which lower both the risk and the height of the inertia barrier for a small organization as compared to a larger one:

- The more informal, open structure of a small organization – particularly non-family or non-owner-managed ones – is more amenable to change than the formal, departmentalized structure of a large organization. Also lacking in small organizations is the potential rigidity of key players. These factors are particularly significant in that they operate not only in the 'forward' direction of helping implement change, but also in the 'backward' direction. Thus, should a wrong decision be taken, it is relatively easy to reverse it. Decisions which can maintain reversibility and not irrevocably commit strategic resources have been found in general to be effective approaches to strategic decision making and organizational learning.
- The *whole* organization is close to the customer. Thus, for example, improvements in turnover that result from a better customer service rapidly permeate through the whole organization. In larger organizations, while the improvements are immediately obvious in the sales and marketing departments, they take longer to permeate back down to, say, the goods-inwards department.

This, though, is clearly not the whole story. Were it so, it would be plausible to expect that a high proportion of management buyouts would give rise to TQM-orientated companies. This does not seem to be the case – as exemplified by the lack of literature references already noted. What, then, are the other factors that tip the balance towards TQM? It is suggested that there are several:

- A management structure. Although it has been implied earlier that a formal, rigid structure can be a barrier to implementing TQM, a complete absence of structure, as happens in many small businesses where the owner 'manages' everything, is an even bigger barrier. The owner is totally involved in the day-to-day operation of the company and does not have time to consider 'non-mainstream' concepts such as TQM.
- A desire to grow. Many small businesses are content to stay at their existing size. Note, for example, how few retail outlets grow into chains. In the grocery trade,

as an instance, there are very few intermediate-size organizations; there are the big chains and the corner shops with very little in between.

- A desire to develop – in the sense of innovating in terms of either product or method of service. This desire can be typified, in Hydrapower's case, by the introduction of the 'Hosemobile' operation.
- A passion for quality. If the basic philosophy of an organization is to be changed, it is essential that everybody in the organization comes to believe in the goal.
- A desire to learn. It is the contention of this chapter that this is the true hallmark of a TQM company: that it is a *learning organization*.

Of these five factors, all but the first are motivational. Seldom are all these latter factors present. A small business may well have a management structure, the desire to grow and develop, and a passion for quality. It is rare, though, for it to have the desire to learn. This is essentially a reflection on the type of person – business rather than management orientated – normally found at the head of a small organization.

An adaptation of force field analysis (Lewin, 1951) is a useful concept in this context. Figure 3.7 shows the balance between the forces driving an organization like Hydrapower towards TQM and the forces resisting such a move. For an organization to adopt TQM, the sum of the forces on the left of the diagram (the drivers) have to be stronger than the sum of those on the right (the resistors).

It is important to note that the particular balance is specific to a particular point in time. Once the decision is taken to implement TQM, and activities start occurring, the balance changes. That something happens is, in a sense, more important initially than what the something is. It will be recalled that this was one of the findings of the Hawthorne experiment. This was a series of studies conducted in the 1920s and 1930s at Western Electric's Hawthorne plant to examine the effect on productivity of changes in working conditions. The conclusion was that it was the social attitudes and group dynamics that were important and not the physical conditions (see, for example, Whyte 1957). That observers were taking an interest in their operation and seeking to involve them led the workforce to respond positively. It is worth noting, in passing, that a recent study (Jones, 1992) has questioned the statistical validity of the improvement measures.

Provided that the initial action is not seen as counter to the ongoing TQM development, these findings apply equally to the introduction of TQM. If the initial actions are seen to be successful, environmental factors, especially better customer relations, will erode the resisting forces and the TQM programme will develop a momentum of its own. This erosion is more rapid in a small organization than in a large one, due to the greater permeability referred to earlier. Should the implementation fail, the reverse occurs and any attempted relaunch will be that much more difficult. Before considering the ongoing dynamics, though, it is important to examine further, in view of its key importance, the concept of a learning organization.

The learning organization

A learning organization can best be characterized as one that is prepared to experiment. True learning – as opposed to training – comes only from experimentation. The organization learns whether or not the experiment is successful. If it is successful, all well and good: there is an improvement. If the experiment fails, then, and this is the

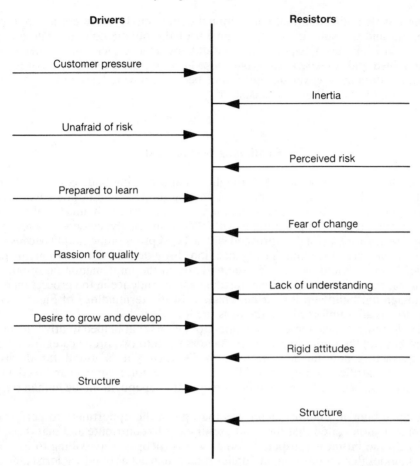

Drivers **Resistors**

Customer pressure

Inertia

Unafraid of risk

Perceived risk

Prepared to learn

Fear of change

Passion for quality

Lack of understanding

Desire to grow and develop

Rigid attitudes

Structure

Structure

Figure 3.7 The TQM force field

key difference between a learning and any other organization, it learns from its mistakes, formulates another experiment and tries again. Kolb (1984) has coined the phrase 'experiential learning' to describe this process, which he terms the Kolb cycle.

A similar concept is that of action learning (Revans, 1979), although this phrase tends to be used more in the formal training context, rooted as it is in the idea that such training should be based on real business experiences rather than on academic theory.

Any TQM implementation is a learning experience, and a learning organization will feel itself to be 'all the better for having tried'. Even those companies which follow one of the quality paths – Deming or Crosby, for example – find themselves in a learning situation when they come to apply the general concepts to their own particular circumstances. Unless they are prepared to experiment, and accept that the consequences will sometimes be failure and the need to re-evaluate, they will not successfully implement TQM.

Hydrapower differs from such 'following' companies only in a matter of degree. There were no role models that fitted its particular situation and so it was forced into the experimentation approach from the start. An excellent example of the company's learning was its realization that conventional quality circles were not an appropriate mechanism and the subsequent development of the bubble concept. There are, no doubt, other examples of experiments that did not achieve their initial objectives and were modified and re-experienced, but these have not been formerly recorded – not through an attempt to cover up, but rather because, having learned from them, the company does not dwell on past mistakes.

Continuing development

Newton's first law of motion states, roughly, that a moving body continues to move providing that there are no external forces acting on it. In the business world things are not that simple. If a TQM programme is to succeed, it must yield financial improvements. If not, the programme will, almost invariably, cease – very few organizations are altruistic enough to proceed with a TQM programme simply because it is a more humane way of running an organization. Provided these improvements occur, and ideally they should begin to accrue early on in the implementation programme, the original risk is seen to have been justified and confidence in the process increases. The momentum builds up for further change. In the terminology of Figure 3.7, the driving forces are reinforced and the resisting forces eroded.

In Hydrapower's case there are a number of factors that helped to drive the process forward beyond the initial stages. These factors fall into two broad categories: human relations factors and financial factors. While this split is useful for descriptive purposes, it is artificial in that, in real life, the two categories interact and feed on each other. In particular, the financial improvements are dependent on the human relations ones.

The main human relations factor was that, given the opportunity to perform, the workforce demonstrated that they had useful ideas to contribute and that these ideas would help the business prosper. In other words, people were willing to accept the responsibilities that empowerment implies rather than act as blind Taylorist automata. This latter concept comes from the so-called 'father of scientific management', F. W. Taylor (1947, but originally published in 1911), whose thesis was that efficiency was maximized by so organizing production that the workers were simply machines in another form. Contrast this with the Hawthorne findings quoted earlier.

That the workforce welcomed empowerment should be no surprise to anybody familiar with the writings of any of the quality gurus, although it was to some of the Hydrapower management team. To quote one of them, 'I had not appreciated the extent to which the workforce already understood where changes were needed.' This is yet another example of experiential learning. One can read something in a textbook or article, but the theory only becomes concrete when whatever is being discussed is actually experienced. This empowerment process is self-reinforcing. The workforce, like management, gain confidence in their own abilities and become eager to experiment further.

The financial factors that helped push TQM forward have already been noted at the start of this chapter – a greater than 50 per cent increase in turnover in a recession.

The interesting question to pose is whether these financial improvements would have occurred had the TQM programme not been implemented. It is an implicit assumption in the TQM literature that there is a causal relationship running from implementation to profit improvement. Although it is not possible to prove this scientifically, there is considerable circumstantial evidence to suggest that the link is valid, at least in this case.

The argument runs as follows. The hose assembly market is highly competitive with little, if any, product differentiation. That Hydrapower has increased its sales, particularly against the background of a recession, implies that it has taken actions that satisfy customer needs to a greater extent than its competitors. It has already been shown that one of the outcomes of the TQM programme has been a strengthening of the company's order-winning criteria through reduced customer returns and improved delivery performance. It is extremely unlikely that these improvements would have occurred had the TQM programme not been implemented – they spring directly out of it. Hence the assumption of a causal relationship.

SMALL COMPANIES AND TOTAL QUALITY MANAGEMENT

Various statements have been made in the preceding sections comparing small organizations with big ones. The aim of this section is to draw these together and examine the question of whether small organizations have any inherent advantages when it comes to implementing TQM. The three factors that need to be examined are customer relations, internal structure and organizational culture. The concepts that will be introduced are those of manoeuvrability, external awareness and change potential.

Customer relations

Most writers on TQM identify the customer as an important player. Garvin (1987) makes this more explicit than most in that he talks about quality being defined from the customer's point of view. He splits the customer's perception of quality into eight dimensions:

- Performance – the primary operating characteristic of the product or service.
- Features – the secondary characteristics of a product or service.
- Reliability – the frequency with which the product or service fails.
- Conformance – the match with specification or pre-established standards.
- Durability – product life.
- Serviceability – the speed, courtesy and competence of repairs.
- Aesthetics – fit and finish.
- Perceived quality – reputation.

The relative importance of each of these dimensions will vary from product to product – this applies as much to the range of products marketed by a single organization as to different products from different organizations, and, but to a lesser extent, from customer to customer. A quality supplier is one which matches its customer's perceptions most closely.

In one sense, a large organization with its greater market research facilities should be in a better position than a small one in this respect. It should be more capable of analysing which of these eight dimensions are the important ones. Supplier size alone, though, is not the important factor. The key to the relationship may be the relative size of supplier and customer. Whereas big organizations are very close to their big customers, they adopt a much more 'take it or leave it' attitude with small ones. It is after all – Pareto rules here as elsewhere – the former which provide the bulk of their turnover. Small organizations are in a different position. The bulk of their turnover comes from customers who are either of similar size or bigger than them. Thus they may pay them more attention, get closer to them, and understand better their require-ments. This closeness will be reinforced by the nature of the product or service that a small organization provides. This is less likely to be a standard product than in the case of a large organization.

In this respect, therefore, it can be argued that it is easier for a small organization to become a quality supplier than for a large one. This is particularly so if the organiza-tion evolves into a specialist niche supplier. It is interesting to note that Hydrapower has done exactly this. It has expanded from supplying standard hose assemblies into supplying assemblies made to customer-specific requirements. The launch of the 'Hosemobile' service is a continuation of the pattern. Both these moves have forced the company closer to the customer. Ironically, it took these steps only after gaining the initial confidence that the first stages of the TQM programme generated – yet another example of TQM building on itself.

An important aspect of customer relations is that of product profitability. Large organizations have a bigger cushion than smaller ones in this respect. They can trade unprofitably for a far longer period than can small organizations – the latter will soon have their bank manager breathing down their neck. It is extremely doubtful that a quality relationship will be built up, or survive, in an unprofitable situation. Thus large organizations might well not have the incentive to move towards quality even though, in the longer term, this would correct the very problem they currently have.

Given the apparent importance of customer relations, it is notable that Hydra-power did not launch its customer survey until late 1992 – almost two years after the start of the TQM process. The implication is that, while the initial moves stemmed from general evidence from within the customer base of the potential for competitive advantage through quality, there are further advantages still to be exploited.

Internal structure

Typically, large organizations may be seen as bureaucratic, small companies as flex-ible. A useful concept here is that of 'manoeuvrability'. Because managers in small organizations have their roles less rigidly defined, they are freer to take action than their compatriots in larger organizations. Change can be implemented at a far faster rate. Manoeuvrability applies to external as well as internal change and can, perhaps, be seen as the concept underlying what is commonly referred to as 'customer aware-ness'. Bureaucratic organizations, on the other hand, may well suffer from inertia. Once set on a particular course they find it difficult, and slow, to change direction. These are precisely *not* the characteristics that make for a TQM organization. In order to implement TQM it is necessary to put bureaucracy in the background. This can happen, as witness the large, formerly bureaucratic, organizations that have done so. Examples abound, and some are given in this book.

On the other hand, some structure is necessary, particularly if the organization decides to approach TQM via the quality assurance route. A completely unstructured organization would find it very difficult to implement TQM. Recall the comment of Hydrapower's managing director regarding the importance of the company's formal structure as a basis for its expansion. Had that formal structure not been in place, it can be argued that the quality initiatives would not have occurred. A function of structure can be said to be that it allows what might be termed 'change potential' to surface. Change potential can be defined as the unfulfilled desire for change that can build up in any organization. While this desire for change might well be present in both structured and unstructured situations, it can be argued that without a formal structure – a framework the potential can act on – the desire becomes dissipated and the change potential erodes.

A further effect of the organizational structure is to set limits on the degree of action an employee can take, either alone or in conjunction with colleagues, without referring upwards – in other words, the extent to which the employee is empowered. It is worth noting, as an aside, that empowerment is sometimes thought of as an on/off situation – an employee is either fully empowered or not empowered at all – but this is oversimplistic. Empowerment should not be seen as the same as manoeuvrability. The former is internal to the organization; the latter can be internal or external.

In organizational terms, the question thus translates to one of whether it is easier for a large organization to let go of the reins and give more responsibility to its workforce than it is for an undermanaged company to put in the necessary controls – but without destroying its management's manoeuvrability. There is no simple answer to this. Essentially it is a cultural problem.

Company culture

As has already been demonstrated, managers of small organizations are prepared to take risks. It is probably fair to say that they are less risk averse than their equivalents in large organizations. Since the adoption of a TQM philosophy is a risk strategy, it might be expected that small organizations would be more likely to take this path than large ones. This does not, however, appear to be the case. The reason is, perhaps, that a TQM philosophy implies a different type of risk from that inherent in, for example, a management buyout. The obvious focus of the difference is the special types of risk associated with setting up a learning organization. This requires confidence in one's abilities to manage a different type of organization, one which might well 'bite back'. Whereas managers of small organizations are confident in their abilities with respect to commercial decisions, and hence are prepared to take risks, they are less confident when it comes to organizational ones.

Managers of large organizations, on the other hand, can be seen to be in the reverse situation – confident about organizational aspects, less so about commercial risk taking. It is significant in this context that the trigger for adopting TQM in a considerable number of large organizations is a crisis situation. It can be argued that in such a situation risk aversion, and particularly aversion to commercial risk, is reduced. Something *has* to be done, and the organizational possibilities, including TQM, are considered.

TQM is a holistic process. It involves the whole workforce, not just senior management. There is no reason to suppose, though, that the employees in a small organization will react any differently from those in a large one. What could be different is the expectations that managers of large and small organizations have of their workforces in terms of how they will respond to a TQM programme. Managers of large organizations, particularly those that would consider the TQM approach, tend to have a better managerial education and thus are more aware of the response to be expected from their workforce. Small organization managers are not as aware – thus heightening the risk they are taking.

These differences in attitude to risk taking between managers of small and large organizations can be attributed to the different cultures that exist in the two types of organization. There are a number of reasons for these differences, the most important of which are as follows:

- The organizational structure of small organizations results in less fractionated, broader-based staff. There is a tendency for multi-functionality to be the rule rather than the exception.
- Small organizations generate closer relationships, both within staff and between staff and management.
- Small organizations tend to be more 'externally aware'. One manifestation of this is their greater customer awareness. It may well be that large organizations just plough their own furrows and are not responsive to potential change – they may resist learning. Large organizations may remain insular and establish 'defensive routines' which effectively ensure that they cannot change their practices.
- Hickson (1986) has shown that key decisions frequently have significant political overtones. It may well be that the required internal brokering is easier to achieve in a smaller organization.
- There may be more scope for charismatic leadership and intuitive decisions in small organizations. The plethora of checks and balances in large organizations can impede innovation.
- The culture of small companies could well be easier to manage. The culture issue thus becomes a less important factor in the decision-making process.

Summary

There are, as we have seen, both potential advantages and potential disadvantages for small as compared to large organizations in terms of adopting and implementing a TQM programme. They relate to the initial adopton decision rather than the implementation process itself. Once implemented, a successful TQM programme such as that of Hydrapower builds on itself.

The three concepts that have been identified as underlying the differences between small and large organizations are manoeuvrability, external awareness and change potential. Figure 3.8 is an attempt to model the TQM adoption and implementation process in terms of these concepts.

As can be seen from the diagram, external awareness and change potential, together with motivation, which was shown earlier to be an essential ingredient of the mix, generate a climate which makes the organization a potential candidate for TQM. It is our contention that it is the third concept, manoeuvrability, that brings about the transition from potential to actual. An important component of this model is the positive feedback loop. As noted earlier, an important TQM driver is the success of the initial experiments. In terms of this model, success reinforces the driving factors by building confidence, and this, in turn, carries the process further forward.

This model is as yet untested. It may be incomplete. Additional factors may well need to be added to explain the differences between large and small organizations in terms of TQM take-up. The analysis carried out in this chapter suggests that smaller

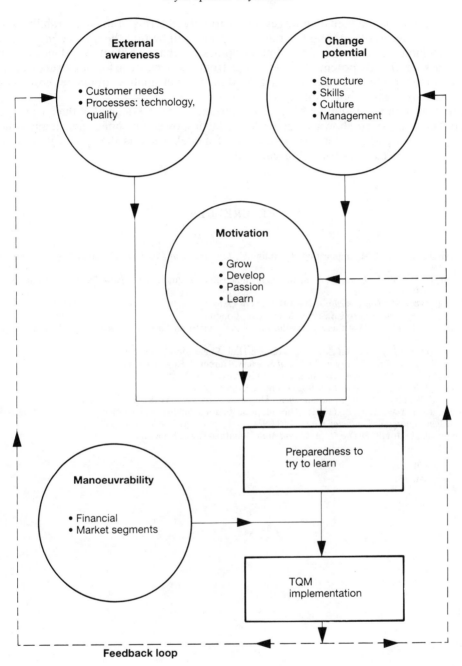

Figure 3.8 TQM: a conceptual model

organizations rate higher than larger ones certainly in terms of manoeuvrability and, perhaps, in terms of external awareness. It could well be that the missing ingredients which inhibit the adoption of TQM philosophies are change potential and motivation. The lack of change potential could result from the lack of a formal structure; the motivational problem could well relate to difficulties in smaller companies embracing the learning organizational ethos.

In view of the vast number of small organizations in the UK, and of the advantages that TQM has been shown to generate in Hydrapower Dynamics and many other companies, exploration and development of models such as that postulated above could well prove a very fruitful research area.

REFERENCES

Brown, A. (1992) 'TQM: Implications for training', *Industrial and Commercial Training*, vol. 24, no. 10, pp. 3–9.

Garvin, D. A. (1987) 'Competing on the eight dimensions of quality', *Harvard Business Review*, Nov./ Dec., pp. 101–9.

Hickson, D. (1986) *Top Decisions*, Basil Blackwell, Oxford.

Hill, T. (1985) *Manufacturing Strategy*, Macmillan, London.

Jones, S. R. G. (1992) 'Was there a Hawthorne effect?', *American Journal of Sociology*, vol. 98, no. 3, pp. 451–68.

Kolb, D. (1984) *Experimental Learning*, Prentice-Hall, Englewood Cliffs, NJ.

Lewin, K. (1951) *Field Theory in the Social Sciences*, Harper & Row, New York.

Porter, M. E. (1985) *Competitive Advantage*, Free Press, New York.

Revans, R. W. (1979) *Action Learning*, Blond & Briggs, London.

Taylor, F. W. (1947) *Scientific Management*, Harper & Row, New York.

Whyte, J., and Witcher, B. (1992) 'The adoption of total quality management in northern England', Durham (quoted in *Financial Times*, 14/11/92).

Whyte, W. H., Jr (1957) *The Organisation Man*, Jonathan Cape, London.

FOUR

ICL KIDSGROVE:
Snapshot of a changing culture

NICK JOHNS
AND
JOHN CHESTERTON

FOUR

ICL Kidsgrove:
Snapshot of a changing culture

The process of installing quality improvement is a journey that never ends. Changing a culture so that it never slips back is not something that is accomplished quickly. Nothing happens just because it is the best thing to do, or just because it is worthwhile ... we have to describe the future as we would like it to be and then march on down the yellow brick road.
Philip B. Crosby, *Quality without Tears*, 1984

INTRODUCTION

International Computers Ltd (ICL) is one of the most successful British information technology companies, yet during the early 1980s it teetered on the brink of bankruptcy. One of the management innovations which saved it was a company-wide quality improvement process. This chapter describes the development and operation of ICL's quality management system at grass-roots level: The Kidsgrove Manufacturing Operation.

ICL KIDSGROVE

Origins of ICL

Development of computer technology in the UK began during the Second World War. Research groups, of mainly university personnel, were set up by the Ministry of Defence to produce electronic calculating machines for cracking enemy codes. After the war these academics took their projects back to the universities. A number of peacetime research teams were formed and several British computer prototypes began to take shape.

In the late 1940s, computers were very cumbersome affairs. Solid-state electronics had not yet been invented, so the technology of the time required large numbers of thermionic valves. Accommodating, maintaining, linking and cooling them needed a high standard of technical expertise. Thus in due course all of the viable computer projects became jointly financed, collaborative ventures between the university/ research sector and the electrical engineering industry. During the 1950s five independent prototypes established themselves in this way and limited production of some machines began.

The first British computers were expensive novelties and as such had few ready buyers. Manufacturers soon found that it was not enough to master the new production technology. The product itself required considerable marketing expertise, which was not always available. During the 1960s the five commercial interests resolved themselves into two, one of which was the System 4 machine, produced by English Electric. The other, the 1200/1900 series, was produced by the British Tabulating Machine Company (BTM), which in 1958 became International Computers and Tabulators (ICT). The BTM/ICT development group was larger and more market orientated than English Electric, but neither company grew quickly enough to compete in the international computer market.

The policy of the Labour government during the late 1960s was to encourage mergers within British industry, as a response to foreign competition. British computers, rapidly losing their market share to US imports, were seen as a prime candidate for such a merger. ICT and English Electric at first strongly resisted government pressures, but eventually the new Ministry of Technology managed to negotiate a merger. Shareholders of ICT received 53.5 per cent of the new company, two 18 per cent shares were acquired by English Electric and Plessey (which had made a last-minute cash bid), and the government bought the remaining 10.5 per cent with a cash injection of its own. The resulting new company, International Computers Limited (ICL), came into being in 1968 (Moralee, 1981).

Production strategy

After the merger ICL was left with two products, both mainframe computers. The 1900 series had been inherited from BTM/ICT and the System 4 from English Electric. The computer market at that time was already dominated by IBM, which had adopted a very effective product strategy based on the compatibility of its different models. Its '360' range of machines offered complete upwards compatibility. In other words, software which worked on a basic machine was guaranteed to run when a customer wished to upgrade to a more expensive IBM model. IBM policy also featured forward compatibility, i.e. software from older models would run on newer ones as they became available. As the cost of software rose, customers became increasingly reluctant to 'trade up' to a non-IBM machine, for which a whole new set of operating material would need to be written. This product strategy eventually gained IBM the lion's share of the world hardware market. Several of its competitors also began to produce IBM-compatible machines to cash in on an increasingly standardized market.

ICL's 1900 series was not IBM compatible, but had its own 'captive' market, mostly in the UK. System 4 was IBM compatible. It was also more flexible than the 1900. For example, it would work more effectively 'on line' through a terminal than the 1900, which was basically a card/tape machine. During the late 1960s, however, IBM began an aggressive strategy of price cutting, and several competitiors offering compatible machines were driven out of business. The viability of the System 4 was seriously threatened, and in 1970 ICL made the decision to develop a new product line, the 2900 series. This was to outclass IBM's products in flexibility, but to have its own internal compatibility, avoiding IBM compatibility as a matter of policy. The first sophisticated new 2900 models, in production by 1974, were unfortunately not compatible with either the 1900 series or System 4. They also suffered a number of teething troubles which, together with the compatibility problems, lost ICL numerous customers. To make matters worse, the company was very slow to release an emulator package.

Emulator software enables one model of computer to perform as if it were another. The 2900 series was so powerful that it could be made to emulate the 1900, and in this way established customers could run their old software on the new machines. However, emulators occupy a lot of memory. A 2900 machine emulating a 1900 lost much of its power and flexibility. Emulator facilities were therefore deliberately withheld to encourage customers to gain maximum advantage from their new machines. This policy lost ICL more of its existing customers.

Between 1968 when ICL was formed and 1974, the year the 2900 series was launched, a revolution occurred in the computer world. Developments in chip technology and the growing sophistication of printed circuit boards suddenly opened up an enormous new market by making it possible to produce personal computers and smaller business systems. During this period, ICL had committed virtually all of its resources to the 2900 mainframe series and had overlooked or ignored the new areas which were being exploited by its competitors. Fortunately, the company was able in 1974 to acquire Singer Business Machines, a subsidiary of a US company specializing in small business systems. Singer's business grew rapidly, providing one-third of ICL's total turnover by 1980. However, the company continued to devote its development resources to the 2900 series. The technology of the Singer product, known as System 10, thus became increasingly outdated compared with its competitors.

Difficulties at ICL

Like other company mergers secured by the British government during the late 1960s, ICL suffered problems of internal coherence. It was a typical example, composed of separate companies located at separate sites and with their own separate products. Inevitably, there was product chauvinism, with internal battles for development and marketing resources. There was also compartmentalization between the various sites, which had developed their own cultures before the merger and continued to cling to them afterwards. Singer's purchase in 1974 and its rapid growth in turnover exacerbated the existing problem, which resulted in poor internal communications and patchy management control.

The culture at ICL during the 1970s tended to value technical expertise more highly than marketing or strategic planning. Most managers were technical or engineering specialists, who had been promoted up through the line organization. Although market awareness had been the key to BTM's growth and to the eventual formation of ICL, by 1980 there was little recognition of this within the management structure. Business attitudes within ICL were directed towards the product (primarily the 2900 mainframe series) rather than towards the customer. Hence the company's marketing approach was to make more-or-less general purpose hardware, for which it assumed customers would find a use. There was no attempt to identify individual customers' needs or to direct the corporate imagination towards new applications. ICL saw itself as a provider of a technologically excellent product, not as a solver of customers' problems. In effect there was no overall marketing strategy. Such commercial success as the company possessed had been achieved in a piecemeal way. Some of the products contributing to it, such as the System 4 and Singer's System 10, were actually regarded in a 'Cinderella' light because they were peripheral to the perceived main thrust: 1900 and 2900 series mainframes. Managers generally felt that their products were technically equivalent, or even superior, to those of its competitors. However much this might have been justifiable on engineering grounds, the company's production capacity, marketing and business strategy lagged far behind those of their major competitors. This arrogant attitude to the technology merely distorted the company's business perspective.

By 1981 ICL had lost a substantial number of its original 'captive' mainframe customers. Its market share had dwindled to a small fraction of that in 1971 and it relied for its custom more and more on the UK public sector. Despite the acquisition of Singer in 1974, and the comparatively good sales of the smaller 2900 series models, ICL had almost been squeezed out of the lucrative microcomputer and mini-system market. The product range was unsteady owing to teething troubles, compatibility problems and fragmentation within the company. As a result, turnover slumped and in 1981 ICL made a pre-tax loss of £50 million.

Rescue from the brink

At this point the government, still an ICL shareholder from the 1968 merger, stepped in with a rescue deal. The company received a £200 million guaranteed loan and a new management team was appointed. Christopher Laidlaw became president and Dr Robb Wilmot was recruited from Texas Instruments as managing director. Tough new cost control measures were immediately imposed in order to reduce the loss. The total workforce was cut by one-third to 22,000 across the company. Inventory was drastically reduced and new budgetary and management systems were introduced. ICL immediately began to make a modest profit (see Figure 4.1).

Wilmot believed that people and attitudes, rather than cuts and controls, were the real key to saving the company. Many of the original ICL managers were replaced with new blood from other companies. For example, Peter Bonfield, who eventually succeeded Wilmot as managing director, was recruited from Texas Instruments. Education was identified as the way to change attitudes within the company. In 1982 G. Hamel of the London Business School and C. K. Pralahad of the University of Michigan were approached to put together a training programme in strategy and marketing for ICL's senior management. During 1983 and 1984 the company ploughed 10 per cent of its profits into management training, which produced immediate results. For example, the marketing director soon focused the attention of the sales force on to 1,000 strategically important customers in specialized markets, producing a 30 per cent increase in orders by 1985. Strategic decisions also quickly made their way into all divisions of the company.

Robb Wilmot quickly realized the importance of changing the focus of ICL's strategy away from technological 'boxes' and towards a customer-led approach. At first he attempted to impose his attitudes on the company by means of a stream of memos and policy documents, which became known by his colleagues as 'Robbo-grams'. There were also deliberate attempts to change the culture by producing documents such as 'The ICL Way' (summarized in Table 4.1). This document has since become an important instrument of company culture, but it was received cynically at the time as the clumsy attempt of an outsider to manipulate attitudes. Eventually, on the advice of an industrial psychologist, Wilmot realized that

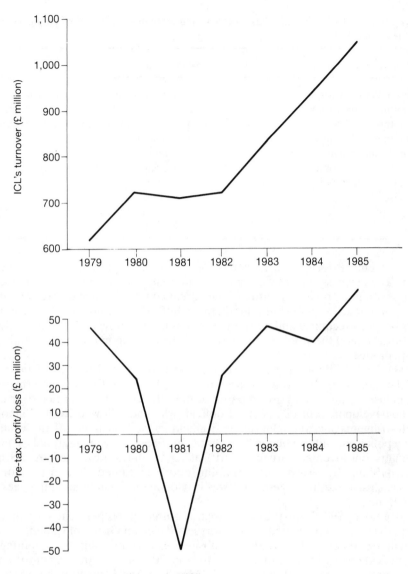

Source: Adapted from Lorenz (1986).

Figure 4.1 ICL's turnover and profitability, 1979–1985

attitudes would not change unless he took a more democratic approach to decision making.

Throughout 1983 and 1984 a bottom-up strategic planning process was introduced to identify ongoing changes that needed to be made within the company. A parallel review of organization and management was also initiated, so that necessary changes could be put into practice within the company.

During 1984, Wilmot made further changes in the organizational structure of ICL. Interdisciplinary 'business centres' were created, dedicated to each of the company's

Table 4.1   Summary of 'The ICL Way' – seven commitments expected of all employees and 10 management obligations

Commitments of employees	Management obligations
1. Commitment to change	1. Business manager = people manager
2. Commitment to customers	2. Direction: objectives and strategies
3. Commitment to excellence	3. Strategic thinking exploiting change
4. Commitment to teamwork	4. High-value outputs
5. Commitment to achievement	5. Teamwork
6. Commitment to people development	6. Development of employees
7. Commitment to creating a productivity showcase	7. 'Can-do' attitude
	8. Innovation
	9. Recognizing and facing difficult issues
	10. Self-measurement

market segments. Priority was given to the needs of major customers such as the retail industry. The business centres were largely autonomous and could adopt independent strategies within the policy structure of the parent company. Each centre contained its own development, support and marketing staff, thus removing distinctions and barriers between technical and marketing personnel. In this way the democratic ethos was reinforced, and the whole organization was focused upon the market, rather than upon the product.

In 1984 Robb Wilmot left ICL to set up a new company, European Silicon Structures. The same year, ICL was acquired by STC plc, which thus became the second-largest industrial electronics group based in the UK. However, the takeover did not affect the development of ICL. Peter Bonfield, who had followed Robb Wilmot from Texas Instruments, became chairman. Bonfield carried on many of the changes in company policy and culture begun by Wilmot. In 1986 he also inaugurated a company-wide quality improvement process (QIP) along the lines advocated by US quality consultant Philip B. Crosby. The training effort continued, but instead of being devoted exclusively to management it was broadened to include all employees in the organization.

In November 1990, Fujitsu Ltd of Japan acquired an 80 per cent shareholding in ICL, with STC Ltd, now owned by the Northern Telecom Group of Canada, retaining the remaining 20 per cent. ICL and its subsidiaries currently supply computing hardware, applications software and services to over 70 countries throughout the world. Joint venture companies with Fujitsu and KMECS (in the Tatar Republic) service the North American and Russian subcontinents respectively, and in 1991 ICL further strengthened its international base by merging with the Finnish company Nokia Data. ICL regards Europe as its home market and plans to be the leading supplier in its field in the 1990s. The company's policy is to increase turnover and market share by means of acquisitions, mergers and joint ventures wherever these fit its business strategy.

Manufacturing division: Kidsgrove and Ashton

Figure 4.2 shows the functions and subsidiaries which make up the ICL organization. ICL's main manufacturing facilities are located in the UK, in Continental Europe

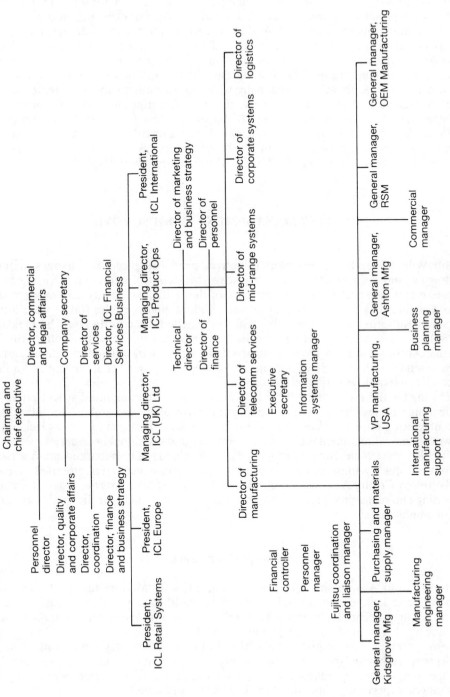

Figure 4.2 ICL organization chart as at autumn 1992

(including Russia) and in India. The manufacturing division within the UK consists of four operations, centred around two principal sites. Printed circuit boards for all ICL systems are produced at the Kidsgrove site, which also makes boards under contract for external customers. The Ashton plant assembles and tests mainframe, mid-range and personal computers. Both operations make extensive use of just-in-time (JIT) and flexible manufacturing techniques; all machines are built to order, to keep inventory costs to a minimum. During 1990 ICL became the first information technology organization in the UK to achieve company-wide registration to the ISO 9001 quality systems standard. Within the company, the manufacturing division has consistently led the way in quality improvement. Kidsgrove achieved ISO 9002 registration in 1988. In 1990 the Ashton plant won one of only three British Quality Awards from the British Quality Association, and in 1992 Kidsgrove was a finalist for the Perkins Award of the National Society for Quality through Teamwork (NSQT).

QUALITY MANAGEMENT AT KIDSGROVE

Robb Wilmot's early management initiatives produced profound changes at both Kidsgrove and Ashton sites. The innovative stock control and manufacturing techniques mentioned above were one instance of this. Effective quality management was also recognized to be crucial to future success, and quality circles (QCs) were introduced at Kidsgrove as early as 1983. Circles matched the criteria given by Oakland (1989), i.e. they were encouraged to form spontaneously. They met voluntarily, in normal working time, to identify, analyse and solve work-related problems and to recommend solutions to management. A steering group was set up on site and a full-time QC facilitator was appointed.

During the three years from 1983 to 1986, the QC system matured at Kidsgrove. A wide range of problems were solved, from 'no soap in the toilets' to substantial manufacturing projects. However, it also became clear that quality circles lacked the power to make fundamental changes beyond site and divisional boundaries.

In 1986, under the chairmanship of Peter Bonfield, ICL embarked upon a company-wide quality improvement process (QIP). Senior managers attended courses delivered by Crosby Associates Inc. Structures were set up across the organization for assessing and managing quality, and arrangements were made for the quality training of all employees.

The quality mission

Kidsgrove and Ashton sites share a common mission: 'Manufacturing Division will generate competitive edge for ICL through the world-class manufacture and procurement of high technology products which exceed our customers' requirements.' Achieving this requires a commitment to quality, cost and service surpassing that of any potential competitor. The QIP within manufacturing operations such as Kidsgrove embodies the ICL total quality policy, which states: 'We will provide competitive systems, products and services which fully meet our internal and external customers' expectations first time, on time, and every time.'

Crosby doctrines point the way to achieving both the mission and the quality policy, and they are central to ICL's quality improvement strategy. For example, the quality improvement drive is referred to as a 'process', never as a 'programme'. A 'process' need never end, but the word 'programme' implies something that will eventually finish and be superseded. Like Crosby, ICL defines quality as 'conformance to customers' requirements'. Consequently quality is measured not just in terms of indices or metrics, but as the price of non-conformance (PONC), i.e. the cost of getting it wrong. The company is committed to calculating non-conformance in money terms. This also permits an instant calculation of the savings when a problem is corrected.

Fundamental to ICL's quality improvement process are Crosby's 14 steps of quality improvement, shown in Table 4.2. Company literature represents the steps as jigsaw

Table 4.2   The 14 steps of quality improvement

1	Management commitment	8	Employee education
2	Quality improvement team	9	Zero defects day
3	Measurement	10	Goal setting
4	Cost of quality	11	Error cause removal
5	Quality awareness	12	Recognition
6	Corrective action	13	Quality councils
7	Zero defects planning	14	Do it over again

Source: Adapted from Crosby (1984), p. 99.

pieces making up the quality improvement process. The steps also form a standing checklist of activities. For example, designated 'stepholders' report regularly at team meetings, on their areas of responsibility: error cause removal, employee education, cost of quality, etc. The influence of the 14 steps is clearly visible in the quality improvement structure and culture throughout ICL.

The QIP is allowed to develop simultaneously company-wide and at a local level. For example, education programmes may be initiated by ICL company policy or from within a particular division, in response to identified local needs. Quality strategy at Kidsgrove is similarly based on a combination of the company strategy and local requirements, and is updated yearly. Although strategy at Kidsgrove specifically deals with production processes, quality initiatives affect all aspects of the organization. For example, they extend to employee's health and welfare and to the quality of working life. An important part of the quality strategy at Kidsgrove is to involve customers: not only in-company customers like the Ashton plant, but also external customers, who contributed about one-third of Kidsgrove's total revenue in 1991. Customers' representatives are included in the QIP and regularly participate in the meetings of quality teams.

Quality team structures

The quality team structure at Kidsgrove, shown in Figure 4.3, is broadly based around line management structures. Development of the quality process and strategy is steered by the quality improvement support team (QIST), led by the director of manufacturing and his direct reports. The site quality improvement team (QIT) is chaired by Kidsgrove's general manager and leads the quality improvement process throughout the plant. Corrective action teams (CATs) are formed by management

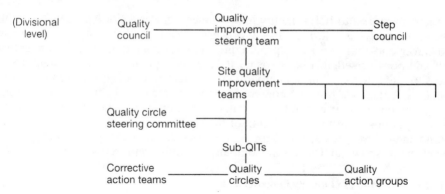

Figure 4.3   Quality teams: manufacturing division

and report to the site QIT. QCs, on the other hand, are driven by the workforce. In this way, flexibility and democratic ownership are achieved at all levels of the organization, within the constraints of the management structure. Functions and structures of the various teams are discussed below.

Working cultures always tend to develop their own jargon. Crosby-style quality improvement jargon consists of a multitude of acronymic abbreviations, such as PONC (the price of non-conformance) mentioned above. The quality teams shown in Figure 4.3 mostly have their own acronyms, which are used by Kidsgrove staff in everyday speech. Company literature is full of them, which makes it hard to read. Even the site itself is frequently referred to as KMO (Kidsgrove Manufacturing Operations). The newcomer, expressing alarm at yet another acronym, is reassured: 'Don't worry, it's only another TLA.' In the vernacular of ICL Kidsgrove, this stands for three-letter abbreviation. A glossary with brief explanations of these abbreviations is provided at the end of this chapter.

Quality circles

Quality circles were introduced at ICL's manufacturing sites in 1983, three years before the Crosby-style QIP was initiated. By 1986, Kidsgrove already had considerable experience in managing circles, but the number of active QCs did suffer a decline in the early days of the QIP. Their place in the new order was at first poorly understood by the workforce, and there was a feeling that the new teams introduced to implement the QIP would take over the functions of QCs. This misapprehension has since been dispelled and QC members are again on the increase (see Table 4.3).

QCs allow the workforce opportunities to improve the quality of processes and products with which they are involved. The keynotes are employee ownership and empowerment. At Kidsgrove, QCs consist of voluntary groups of employees engaged in similar work. Their brief is to identify and resolve processing problems within the particular department to which they belong. They do not have to include a member of management, but many circles do prefer to include a supervisor, because this helps them get quicker action in solving problems. Any group of workers may form a QC and they have a mandatory right to meet during working hours. However, because of the strain this could put on production, they are expected to negotiate meeting times with their supervisor. The QCs tend to have fanciful names, reflecting the department

Table 4.3   Summary of quality circle status at Kidsgrove in 1991

	No. of circles		No. of members	
Department	1990	1991	1990	1991
Product and material supply (PMS)	5	6	28	31
Printed circuit preparation (PPC)	7	11	54	87
Printed circuit assembly (PCA)	6	6	50	51
Engineering	5	2	28	8
Information systems	3	5	12	15
Site services	0	1	0	9
Finance	1	2	2	2
Personnel	1	1	2	2
Quality	3	2	17	8
Product information	1	1	10	10
Totals	32	37	203	223

or activity. Examples are: '007 Bond' in the bonding area and 'The Happy Forkers' (fork-lift operators). 'The Naughty Bits' is a group engaged in the drilling area, while 'Amber' is named from the lights in the photoprint unit.

QCs form and break up spontaneously. Their dynamics are complicated and depend upon social forces ('If you aren't in it, I don't want to be in it') as well as identified work problems. There is no maximum or minimum stipulated number of members, and QCs may be anything between three and 12 strong. The level of participation is one of Kidsgrove's foremost quality management concerns. During 1991 the number of circles rose from 32 to 37 (see Table 4.3). The proportion of the workforce involved went up from 20 per cent to 23 per cent, facilitated by local management focus and review. It is estimated that about 70 per cent of Kidsgrove employees have been involved in a quality circle at some time.

An early problem at Kidsgrove was the resistance of supervisors and middle managers, who tended to see quality circles as undermining their authority, disrupting work schedules and wasting production time. Middle managers would sometimes forbid meetings or fail to attend them when asked. During the 1980s a significant part of the site QC facilitator's role consisted of persuading supervisors of the value of the circles. As well as promoting diplomacy between workforce and managers, the facilitator also encouraged and developed QC members and helped them to develop their skills. The expertise and competence of QCs has been further supported by requiring all staff to attend training programmes in problem-solving, teamwork and presentation skills. QCs normally identify and solve problems unaided. For example, in 1990 a circle known as 'The Press Gang' (working the opposite shift to '007' in the bonding area) decided to redesign their work clothing. Overalls soiled quickly and tended to catch and tear on machinery, so they designed close-fitting work tunics with fasten-down cuffs and matching trousers. These remained clean longer, possessed pockets in which notes and tools could safely be stored, and eliminated many of the health and safety hazards of the original workwear.

Occasionally, Kidsgrove circles are asked to take on problems identified elsewhere in the organization. For example, in 1991 ICL manufacturing division decided to replace its solvent-based photographic processing solutions with water-based ones, on grounds of health, safety and cost. Kidsgrove engineering department devised a modified process based on the new chemicals, and then contacted the photoprinting section for its advice on trying out the modified system. The section responded by handing over the problem to its QC 'Amber', which successfully completed the trials and introduced the new process.

Much of the work of QCs is aimed at reducing inefficiency, often with conspicuous savings in cost. The 'Dynamics', who inspect and certify boards in the printed circuit assembly department, produced substantial savings during 1990/1 by reviewing their use of labels. Originally, they had employed blank labels, which each inspector hand-stamped with her own details. This was time-consuming, and information stamped on the labels tended to smudge. The 'Dynamics' managed to purchase sets of preprinted labels for less than the cost of the blank ones. They also reviewed their other labelling and packaging procedures, producing an overall saving of £60,000 over an 18-month period.

In 1991 '007 Bond' greatly improved their efficiency by changing their working procedures. Printed circuit boards are made from thin layers of resin-impregnated fibreglass, coated with photo-etched copper. These are carefully aligned, and heated in a vacuum oven to bond them together. Alignment is achieved by binding the layers and insulation material on to prelocated metal pins. The pins are then removed after bonding. Traditionally, this was done with a number of heavy hammer blows, which damaged the pins and introduced a risk of injury. '007 Bond' developed a special tool which protected both the pin and the operator's hand. Besides the avoidance of personal injury, about £14,000 worth of metal pins were saved in the first year of using the new tool. For this work '007 Bond' won one of the annual Michelin Excellence Awards offered to British QCs by the NSQT.

QCs often choose to make a presentation of their work to the QCSC (i.e. senior managers at the Kidsgrove site). They may also present it to their own area manager or supervisor, but there is no formal requirement for them to do this and some circles merely circulate a written report (the minimum obligation). Checking and assisting QC projects is a function of the local QC facilitators, who since 1991 have produced regular status reports on circle activities. Reports are available to the QCSC and to plant/area managers. Circles' actions are under the direct control of management, who must take the decision whether a particular idea should or should not be carried out. QCs which have a supervisor among their number, or present their work to senior managers at the site, improve their chances of achieving their goal. During 1991, however, despite the recession, no QC project was rejected on cost grounds, and managers were able to hold such costs within their budgets.

The error cause removal/corrective action loop

The QC system may be thought of as a 'loop' in which the workforce are able to recognize and take improvement opportunities. At Kidsgrove there is also another type of corrective loop which enables departmental managers directly to eliminate non-conformance errors occurring in their area of influence. This is the error cause removal/corrective action (ECR/CA) loop. Error cause removal (ECR) is a system by which any employee can notify a 'supplier' department of an error or problem occurring in it. The department concerned is then required to solve the problem (remove the error cause) within a negotiated time-span. If the error cause cannot be removed within the agreed time, the department must set up a corrective action team to solve the problem. The ECR/CA action loop provides a powerful means of tackling quality problems that fall outside the scope of QCs because they fall between departments, between sites or within the remit of the management, rather than that of the work-force. The two loops are shown in Figure 4.4.

Employees are encouraged to complete an ECR form whenever they notice a problem. A completed example of such a form is shown in Figure 4.5. The form originator is responsible for sending it to the appropriate person and getting the problem actioned. This includes agreeing a date for correction, which is entered on the form. The individual responsible for correcting the problem must indicate the action taken, and upon completion the originator of the form signs that the error cause has satisfactorily been removed. ECR forms are retained and logged, and appear as a statistic in the monthly management quality reports. For instance, during 1990, 310 ECRs were raised, 291 were closed and at the end of the year six had still not been completed. In 1991 (a more successful year), 583 ECRs were raised and all were completed within the year.

If the originator of an ECR form fails to get a problem satisfactorily resolved, the department must initiate corrective action (CA) by completing a CA form. This is a more complicated form requiring statements by the individual who reports the error cause, by his or her supervisor and by the manager responsible for the non-conforming process. Information requested includes the following:

- The estimated price of non-conformance (PONC).
- A statement of what is going wrong.
- Measures which should be applied to the solution.
- Details of any possible 'short-term fix'.
- Details of the root cause.
- Details of the actions which will be taken to resolve the problem.
- Details of how the solution has been proven.
- The estimated cost of the solution.

Statistics for CA forms are maintained in much the same way as for ECRs. The work of corrective action teams is reported to management at site and divisional level and also to the workforce.

Corrective action teams

CATs represent an essential component of the ECR/CA loop described above. Their members are appointed by management to tackle a specific identified problem. Usually they consist of specialists such as engineers, technicians and managers, depending on the particular needs of the problem, and they are disbanded once the problem has been solved. By contrast, QCs are driven by the needs of the shop floor, as identified directly by the workforce, and membership is voluntary. CATs are therefore a separate quality improvement system driven by management and com-plementary to the QC structure (see Figure 4.3). CATs were introduced at Kidsgrove with the QIP in 1986, and their development as an effective quality tool was not without its problems. At first the workforce perceived them as an alternative to QCs,

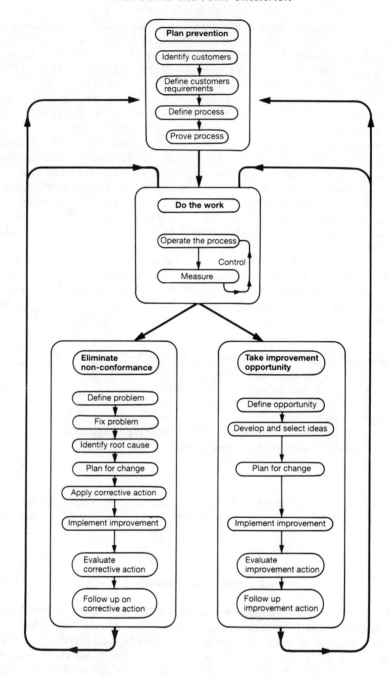

Figure 4.4 The process improvement cycle

```
┌─────────────────────────────────────────────────────────────────┐
│                                                                   │
│  Originator: _____  Extn:_____  Date:_____   │
│                                                                   │
│  Reference no.: _____                         │
│                                                                   │
│                                    Business function              │
│  Department: _____/operation _____         │
│                                                                   │
│  What is the problem?: _____            │
│                                                                   │
│  _____           │
│                                                                   │
│  _____           │
│                                                                   │
│  _____           │
│                                                                   │
│  _____           │
│                                                                   │
│  _____           │
│                                                                   │
│  Actionee: _____  Date received:_____          │
│                                                                   │
│  Agreed forecast completion date:_____           │
│                                                                   │
│  Action taken: _____            │
│                                                                   │
│  _____           │
│                                                                   │
│  _____           │
│                                                                   │
│  _____           │
│                                                                   │
│  _____           │
│                                                                   │
│  Sign off by operator _____  Date_____          │
│                                                                   │
└─────────────────────────────────────────────────────────────────┘
```

Figure 4.5   Example of an error cause removal form

and circle membership fell dramatically until ways were found to improve employees' understanding of the different roles. Another early difficulty, lack of training, disappeared as more employees underwent the mandatory training programmes.

CATs are driven by the need to eliminate a specific PONC, identified in one of several ways. Each department performs regular PONC calculations on identified target areas, and in addition, departments undergo full PONC audits run by the quality department, on a rotating basis. Besides this the ECR/CA loop also provides a means of systematically identifying problems and assigning PONCs to them. CATs must be registered and carefully monitored. Without coordination they achieve little, and sometimes different groups may attempt to tackle the same problem. A designated stepholder, the corrective action coordinator is responsible for checking CAT registration and maintaining records. A monthly progress report is produced on CATs' activities, and CAT statistics are reviewed regularly by management. During 1991 the number of active CATs fluctuated between 151 and 180.

Quality action groups

An issue which emerged while the QIP was being embedded was the need to reinforce the ethos that departments were responsible for quality. At Kidsgrove there had always been some tension between the operation of QCs and maintaining supervisors' authority on the shop floor. This was reinforced by the introduction of CATs. A gulf began to yawn between the latter, which were closely administered by management, and the QC system, which was to a large extent owned by the workforce. Quality action groups (QAGs) were devised to fill the gap. Unlike QCs and CATs, QAGs are specific to ICL. QAG members are appointed by supervisors to monitor quality problems and developments in a particular area. They meet weekly and review the work of both QCs and CATs within the area. They also conduct cost-of-quality exercises and identify problems, and may recommend action through the error cause removal system. Larger problems may be passed on to CATs or QCs. QAGs operate solely within the authority of departmental or area managers. They are not registered like CATs, but their meetings are usually minuted and they may report their actions to senior management through the system of quality improvement teams.

Quality teams at works level

According to Crosby, the second step of the QIP is the quality improvement team (QIT). Each division has its own QIT, under the control of the appropriate director, and within ICL Manufacturing Division there are four QITs at operational level, one of which is Kidsgrove. The site QIT meets monthly under the leadership of the plant manager. Members include departmental managers and the quality improvement support manager, plus the site stepholders. Thus the members of staff responsible for corrective action coordination, quality education, etc. all attend quality improvement team meetings and update their colleagues on progress. The QIT agenda contains standing items which correspond closely to Crosby's 14 steps, as shown in Table 4.4.

Table 4.4   Typical KMO QIT agenda items, and relevant quality steps

Agenda item	Step number*	Step name*
Measurement charts	3	Measurement
	10	Goal setting
Price of non-conformance	4	Cost of quality
Quality initiatives	5	Quality awareness
Corrective actions	6	Corrective action
Zero defects	7	Zero defects planning
	9	Zero defects day
Quality education	8	Employee education
Error cause removals	11	Error cause removal
Recognition process	12	Recognition
Quality circle progress	**	–

* These refer to Crosby's 14 steps of quality (see Crosby, 1984, p. 99).
** Crosby approves of quality circles but tends to play them down, because he wishes to focus management's attention on its own role. Therefore there is no 'quality circle step'.

Area QITs

Soon after the QIP was introduced in 1986, it was discovered that the QIT's wide remit involved it in excessive local detail. Three area QITs were established, one in each of the three largest Kidsgrove departments. These are attended by stepholders, just as at works level. Other members of area QITs are the department manager and the area supervisors. They cover an agenda similar to that of the site QIT itself and can implement any decisions which are within the authority of the departmental managers. The area QITs report to the QIT, to whom any decisions outside their power are referred. QAGs are also in effect subordinate QITs at a still lower level in the organization, but their agendas, structures and reporting duties are much less formalized.

Quality circle steering committee (QCSC)

The present steering committee for QCs at Kidsgrove is the direct descendant of that established in 1983, when circles were first introduced. It consists of the general manager and those who report directly to him. Stepholders are not involved, because the QCSC concerns itself only with the formation, operation and maintenance of QCs. Members receive regular status reports from the site QC facilitator, indicating the numbers, current activities and membership of circles. They also study written reports issued by the circles themselves. QCs are encouraged to present their work to the committee, and can claim a special time allowance for this. Some projects may take a few minutes to explain, but presentations requiring full-scale demonstrations can last hours. The QCSC also underwrites the cost of implementing projects suggested by circles.

Quality teams at divisional level

Site QITs have their own coordinating body at divisional level, analogous to the QC steering committee. This body, the quality improvement steering team (QIST), consists of the director of manufacturing and those who report directly to him. The general manager of Kidsgrove, who heads the Kidsgrove QIT, is therefore a member. The QIST meets monthly and reviews reports from the quality improvement teams. It also receives inputs from the quality council and the step council, which are translated into quality strategy for the division. Thus the QIST sets the pace of the QIP and also ensures that senior management is fully aware of the company's progress in quality improvement.

The step council is concerned with the maintenance of Crosby's 14 steps of quality improvement. Its members are directors and senior managers of ICL who monitor progress in the steps company-wide and decide policy and strategy in each area. The step council concentrates on one quality step at a time: for instance, the council coordinates the various zero defects days at operational units within the division. It is also concerned with recurrent or ongoing steps, such as quality education initiatives and employee recognition.

The quality council, on the other hand, is itself the thirteenth step in Crosby's list. It aims to bring together all those professionally involved in quality improvement within the division. According to Crosby, 'Quality professionals are either actively involved in helping the company eliminate hassle and believe that Zero Defects is indeed achievable, or they are trying to encourage more and more worker motivation and communication programs and to convince top management that Zero Defects is not really obtainable' (Crosby, 1984, p. 119). The quality council helps to focus quality professionals on developments in all the quality steps. It is attended by senior representatives from all divisions, and by senior managers with stepholder roles, rather like the QITs. Meetings are chaired by the director of quality and corporate affairs, a member of the board of ICL.

Educational support

The keynote of ICL's successful corporate development since 1981 has been education. Training programmes were at first largely confined to management, but they were rapidly extended to all employees as their value was realized. Early programmes were concerned with marketing, teamwork and the company mission. The introduction of the QIP in 1986 brought with it a wave of top-down education, focused upon quality. Directors and senior managers attended a five-day programme, the content of which was then disseminated to the rest of the organization on the cascade principle. Selected employees attended a training course qualifying them to deliver Crosby Associates' quality education system. This was the course of 10 weekly three-hour sessions attended by the majority of ICL staff. Non-supervisory staff also received five weekly two-hour sessions to help them apply the principles of quality improvement at the workplace.

The quality education system allowed for very rapid throughput. Company-wide it took just over two years to train 23,000 staff, virtually the whole of the workforce. One clear quality language was established across the whole of ICL, leading to a general understanding of company goals and of the QIP. However, the American-inspired training programme had its disadvantages. The 'razzmatazz' style was difficult for British audiences to relate to, and with only five days' training themselves, the standard of instructors' delivery was somewhat variable.

In July 1987, Kidsgrove was fitted out with special training rooms to cope with the new education programmes. The new centre was christened the Quality Centre. The quality education system took only 18 months to train the 1,500 Kidsgrove staff, but the Quality Centre remains, housing the quality department. All quality education initiatives now take place there, as do many team meetings and some general in-house staff training. Kidsgrove employees continue to see their Quality Centre as tangible evidence of the company's commitment to the QIP.

Quality education can never be a one-off event. It needs continual reinforcement, and 1989 saw the first of ICL's own in-house quality training courses. Entitled 'Quality Improvement for the Individual' (QIFTI), it deals with the need for quality improvement, prevention and corrective action, and the commitment to quality expected of ICL employees. Attendance is mandatory for all employees, from operatives to directors, and lasts full time for two and a half days. During 1990, refresher QIFTI courses were developed, including a special half-day module for managers. These focus on reviewing individuals' progress and helping them to identify practical actions for further quality improvement. Also in 1990 it became apparent that the QC leaders' courses which had gradually been developing since 1983 had now become too cumbersome. The content and time-span needed rationalizing, and there was also an increased demand for training in problem solving, brought about by the introduction of CATs and QAGs. The 'Tools, Techniques and Teamwork' course was developed to meet these needs.

Kidsgrove's management team underwent refresher quality training during 1990, and the majority of the workforce attended specially tailored half-day programmes the following year. However, the increasing flexibility of production facilities has brought training problems due to a large influx of temporary staff. These workers normally sign on for a three-month contract and may not be with the company long enough to attend QIFTI programmes. A one-day course was therefore developed during 1991, designed as part of a standard induction package for new temporary employees. Its objectives are to introduce such staff to the QIP and to take an active part in it.

Quality education is very much a live issue at Kidsgrove. Not only are existing courses continually evaluated, but new programmes are planned, and the likely needs of staff are regularly reviewed. During 1991 planning began on a new series of programmes which will eventually supersede QIFTI. A one-day course for CAT members was also developed, as well as programmes in statistical process control (SPC). The latter is rapidly becoming the standard means of process evaluation at Kidsgrove. ICL is also becoming increasingly concerned with customer care, which is seen as the key to competitive edge during the 1990s. Senior managers at Kidsgrove attend a one-day workshop in customer care during 1991, and all employees attended a half-day event during 1992.

Quality education programmes at Kidsgrove are delivered mainly by members of the quality department. Course delivery has gradually evolved from a more or less content-orientated style in the earlier QIFTI versions to a format which fits the needs of trainees in a more flexible way. For instance, before delivering the half-day management refresher module, the trainer/facilitator is now asked to do the following:

- Send a handbook and video to each attendee and insist that he or she reads/views it.
- Contact the manager and discuss how to introduce the session, how to highlight current departmental performance and which current problem to focus the session on.
- Discover whether the video is relevant for the session, and thus whether to use it.
- Arrange for someone to take minutes of the session.
- Ensure that participants bring their diaries, so that follow-up sessions can be arranged.

The educational mainstay of the quality circles is a programme entitled 'Tools, Techniques and Teamwork' (TTT), introduced in 1990. It lasts two days and is often open to all operatives, subject to availability. The programme begins by explaining the differences between QCs and other quality improvement teams, such as CATs and QAGs. Participants are then introduced to techniques for identifying and prioritizing problems. They practise brainstorming, followed by techniques such as paired comparison which enable them to refine their choice to a single, mutually important work problem. Pareto, cause-and-effect and other analytical techniques are used where a more objective approach to problem selection is required. The TTT course helps participants to describe the problem-solving path and to decide how they will evaluate their progress. It also aims to improve the communication and teamwork skills needed to take part in, organize or control a QC. The TTT course breaks down quality improvement exercises into 20 steps and emphasizes the practical relationship between tools and steps, as shown in Figure 4.6.

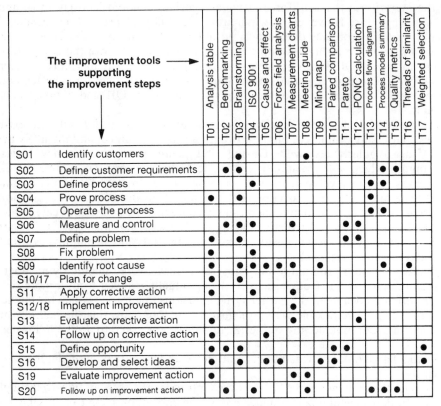

Figure 4.6 The relationship between improvement tools and improvement steps

External education

ICL's QIP requires strong relationships to be maintained with outside suppliers and customers. Kidsgrove's suppliers are regularly audited and their quality management arrangements scrutinized. Since 1991, suppliers who do not have their own quality education arrangements have been requested to attend QIFTI courses. This ensures that suppliers understand Kidsgrove's quality culture and process requirements. ICL is keen to spread the quality gospel further. Quality improvement support managers from Kidsgrove and Ashton have delivered courses to educationalists under the auspices of the Careers Research Advisory Centre (CRAC), a charitable institution sponsored by industry. These 'Quality Management in Education' programmes were based on the QIFTI quality courses, and have received national acclaim. Kidsgrove has also provided quality management input for CRAC's 'Heads Into Industry' programme.

In addition to these courses, ICL Kidsgrove personnel are extensively involved in consultancy. Kidsgrove is one of the founding members of the Central Quality Improvement Network, a loose collaboration of local companies, based at Keele University. The Network's objective is to promote quality improvement in the north-west Midlands, and in particular to help smaller companies. This is mostly done through consultancy visits, meetings and workshops on specific topics, such as the cost of quality. Kidsgrove is also frequently approached by other organizations travelling the quality improvement path. During 1991 over 30 whole-day presentations were requested by a wide range of institutions including British Gas, Cambridge University, BMW and the Bank of South Africa.

Measuring quality

Crosby defines the key measure of quality as the price of non-conformance (PONC). This has been measured at ICL since 1986/7 when the first company-wide audit established a PONC of £162 million. At Kidsgrove the measurement of PONC is carried out in various ways. At departmental level, each manager is expected to identify PONC targets which are calculated and reviewed each month. These measurements are displayed throughout the Kidsgrove plant on special cost-of-quality notice-boards. Reviews of PONC performance quickly highlight manufacturing problems and may lead to the formation of CATs. Because the monthly PONC calculations include only some areas of a department's work, full departmental audits are also undertaken by the quality improvement support manager. About three audits take place each year in rotation, and these may also initiate corrective action.

Another important aspect of the QIP culture is the acceptance that each individual is responsible for the quality of his or her work. All employees at the Kidsgrove plant are encouraged to devise means of measuring their process output and to record these measurements graphically on charts. Workers are encouraged to set their own targets, which are entered on the measurement charts and compared with actual performance. The example shown in Figure 4.7 shows the variations in downtime and repair time for a circuit board testing machine during the last quarter of 1991. The engineer responsible for the machine has set a current non-conformance target of 60 minutes which he aims to beat. However, all figures appearing on the chart are regarded as non-conformance, because the machine has its own preventive maintenance programme. The ultimate goal is that this will remove all need for running repairs, and that the non-conformance target will fall to zero (zero defects).

At Kidsgrove the work of every employee is seen as potentially measurable and chartable. Administration staff have their own systems of conformance criteria. For example, senior managers may measure and record the number of items that accrue unanswered on the site electronic mail, the number of meetings for which they are late or have to cancel, and so on. Individual performances are reviewed at staff appraisal sessions. Chart statistics are circulated to the QIT, and the number of charts in use is regarded as an important indicator of progress in the QIP. During 1991 it increased by 19 per cent, from 444 to 529. Management also monitor the number of charts which indicate performance goals, those which achieve zero defects and those which provide price of non-conformance information.

Quality improvement statistics are summarized in a single report, the quality performance sheet. This is circulated regularly and is reviewed at site QIT meetings. The manufacturing director also uses the sheets to assess and compare quality

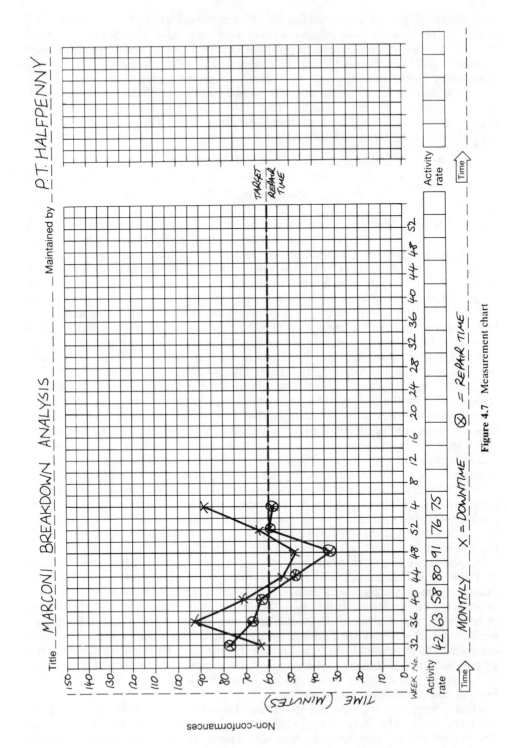

Figure 4.7   Measurement chart

improvement performance at different sites. Quality performance sheets contain the status information on measurement charts described above. They also include statistics of ECR forms and corrective action reports, QC/CAT activity, and recognition nominations and awards. In addition to the quality performance sheets, a monthly quality metrics report is produced and reviewed by site and divisional QITs. The report summarizes the more conventional quality statistics across the division, showing failures in parts per million, as well as PONC. It includes measures of serviceability and ship-to-stock performance.

Employee attitudes are regarded as an important indicator of quality improvement progress. ICL employees' perceptions of the company are regularly surveyed by independent consultants, originally every other year, but annually since 1990. Employees are allowed one hour of work time to complete the extensive opinion survey booklet. Participation is not mandatory, but a 1991 take-up rate of 93 per cent bears witness to the positive employee culture at the Kidsgrove site. Surveys are conducted anonymously and feedback is provided at divisional, site and departmental levels. Any fall in rating from the previous year is carefully noted and investigated, and improvement plans are put in place. Each of the divisional directors' direct reports takes on responsibility for improving one area of negative response. Thus there is a continuous demonstration of management's commitment to quality improvement.

External accreditation is another yardstick by which ICL measures its success. Kidsgrove was accredited by the British Standards Institution with BS 5750 as early as 1984 and the other UK sites followed in 1991. Kidsgrove has also been accredited with the parallel European ISO 9000 series standards. In addition to these general quality accreditations, Kidsgrove also holds a number of product-specific awards. The UL (Underwriters' Laboratories) standard specifies the flammability of products shipped to the USA and involves unannounced inspections four times a year. In 1991 Kidsgrove also received approval from the British Approvals Board Telephones (BABT) covering the manufacture of printed circuit boards for telecommunications. ICL is currently aiming to enter for the European Quality Award, a new quality achievement prize based on a points scoring system similar to that for the US Malcolm Baldridge Award.

Staff appraisal

All ICL staff undergo an annual appraisal during which objectives are set for the year to come. Appraisals emphasize quality issues such as measurement charts, attendance on courses, attitudes and contributions to quality teams. This keeps quality at the forefront and shows individuals exactly how they should be contributing to the QIP. Staff appraisals also offer an opportunity to encourage participation in quality circles, opinion surveys and other voluntary aspects of the QIP.

Management commitment

Management commitment is the first and most important of Crosby's 14 steps. Demonstrating and reinforcing this commitment is essential to morale and to maintaining the QIP. Management commitment is evident in all aspects of quality improvement. Much time and resources are expended on education, on quality teams and on reporting and disseminating information about quality. Both ICL and Kidsgrove have quality magazines. Kidsgrove held a Zero Defects Day on 12 September 1990, on which management and workers made a public commitment to quality. Subsequent years have seen anniversaries of ZDD with displays of current QC projects, which employees are encouraged to view during work time. Management commitment can also be seen in full-time dedicated posts such as the quality improvement support manager. The divisional director keeps in contact with all employees through a regular sheet called the 'Core Brief' and makes himself known to them through quarterly 'kick-off' sessions.

The harmonization programme, which commenced in 1988, demonstrates management's commitment to the development of ICL employees as individuals and as team members. All staff, including hourly paid workers, now enjoy the same working hours, and all salaries are paid monthly. Clocking in and out is no longer required except for those working overtime. The workwear colours which previously differentiated grades of staff have been replaced by universal plain white, marked with individuals' names. Since 1991 Friday has been adopted as 'dressing down day', when all employees can attend work in their normal leisure wear. Single-status staff car parks and restaurants further endorse the harmonization message. 'Them and us' attitudes have begun to give way to a culture in which every Kidsgrove employee is valued as an individual, contributing as a team member to the well-being of the organization. Kidsgrove's general manager reinforces this impression by sending each employee a card on his or her birthday.

Recognition

Like other ICL sites, Kidsgrove has its own mechanism for recognizing individual contributions to the QIP. Any worthy individual or group may be proposed, using a special proposal form. Any member(s) of staff may fill in a proposal form, which is then forwarded to the recognition stepholder. Nominations are reviewed each month with the area QIT stepholders, who agree the award winners; the main criterion is that the award be made for a genuine quality advance and not 'fire-fighting'. Award winners are invited to select a recognition gift from a catalogue issued by the company. Gifts from this catalogue are displayed in cabinets located around the Kidsgrove site. Recipients are presented with their selected gift informally at the workplace, and the presentations are recorded in the monthly quality improvement statistics.

More formal company excellence awards exist, besides the local site-level recognition scheme. These are designated bronze, silver and gold, and recipients receive a certificate and medallion as well as a recognition gift. Examples of work deserving recognition are forwarded to the recognition stepholder, who presents them to the site QIT each month. Those to be recommended for a bronze award are decided and the proposals are sent to the manufacturing division. The divisional QIT then reviews the applications and awards the bronze excellence award against set criteria. Those considered worthy of a silver award are forwarded to the product operations quality improvement team, where they are again reviewed and the awards confirmed. Silver award recommendations are in turn reviewed by Peter Bonfield and the board of ICL, who select those worthy of gold awards.

FUTURE DEVELOPMENTS

ICL's highly successful strategy of customer orientation leads naturally to an increasing emphasis on customer care. Most of ICL's competitors have introduced similar quality improvement strategies, and the quality and reliability of hardware products continues to improve across the market. In addition there has been a worldwide shift to open systems, i.e. towards universal compatibility of hardware and software. ICL itself has spearheaded this movement within Europe. Thus companies no longer have 'captive' markets with expensive software which cannot be run on competitors' machines. Customer care is seen as the key to competitive edge in such a market and is the core of ICL's quality strategy for the 1990s.

Another strategic trend at ICL is the devolution of authority: for example, the manufacturing division became an independent business unit early in 1993. Its mission policy remains unchanged, but it is clear that the division will have two distinct tasks. It is responsible for safeguarding the high quality of hardware so that the company as a whole can concentrate upon gaining competitive edge through customer service. At the same time, manufacturing, like other divisions of the company, is required to develop its own customer care culture.

Kidsgrove is addressing the task of maintaining hardware quality by urging wider use of statistical process control (SPC) techniques. SPC came into use in parts of the processing department during 1991 and spread to the assembly department during 1992. Kidsgrove strategy is to use SPC for the control of every appropriate process by the end of 1993. A key part of this process will be the empowerment of individuals to carry out their own SPC measurements, reflecting the company trend of devolving responsibility. In addition, the manufacturing division is introducing new tools such as Taguchi design methodology. This involves using statistical methods to design products which are less susceptible to processing faults and to produce a more robust product.

There is also a desire at Kidsgrove to encourage greater QC activity. This is partly to balance the increasing emphasis on management quality initiatives such as Taguchi and SPC. But QCs also offer a way to develop customer care initiatives at the site. For example, the idea that courtesy umbrellas should be provided for visitors walking between site buildings originated from a QC. Kidsgrove is currently looking to give its QCs a higher profile through a QC newsletter. Monitoring and reporting of circle activities is being increased, and management are seeking new ways to promote and encourage them.

ICL's culture of concern for customers' needs is reflected in the increasing use of customer satisfaction sheets, for both internal and external customers. During 1991 and 1992 several Kidsgrove departments began issuing satisfaction questionnaires to their internal 'customers', i.e. groups within the organization who use their products. For example, the site facilities department regularly distributes a 21-page questionnaire booklet requiring scaled responses to 98 items. Kidsgrove plans to formalize this survey process, by making it obligatory for all departments and by instituting monitoring and control procedures. A company-wide score-card system was also introduced in 1992, in which customers are invited to score performance in terms of quality, delivery, technology and support. Score-card results are regularly monitored and reviewed. Use of the score-card system continues to grow within ICL and may extend to interdivisional customer relationships as divisional responsibility becomes increasingly devolved.

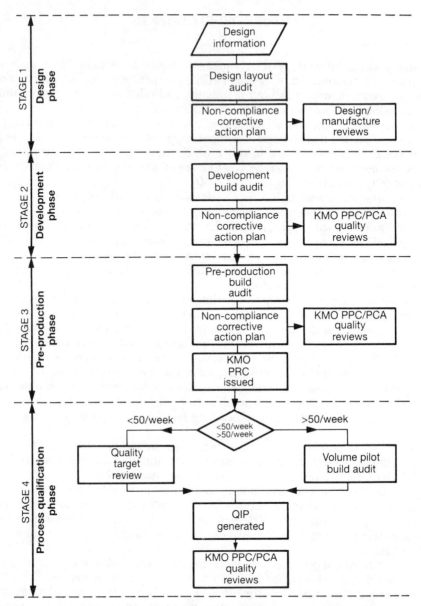

Figure 4.8   Kidsgrove Manufacturing product introduction: quality procedure process flow diagram

New educational initiatives are planned, to support company and divisional strategy. Company training programmes in customer care have been developed, and all ICL personnel will attend them within the next two years. Managers at site and divisional level underwent customer care training during 1992. The company has also developed a successor programme to QIFTI, which is due to supersede the original course during 1993. In this way, the existing quality improvement thrust will be revitalized and strengthened, thus maintaining manufacturing quality as a live issue.

Courses being developed at divisional level emphasize statistical techniques, and SPC training has also been integrated into staff induction packages. The TTT programme is being revised and now includes SPC techniques and their use in self-monitoring at the workplace. A new initiative has been the development of computer-based learning (CBL) software so that SPC skills can be acquired, practised and reinforced at individuals' different learning rates.

Advances in quality monitoring also reflect the growing importance of SPC, and here too supporting software has been developed. For example, an innovative quality modelling system now simulates process quality performance and compares this with actual product results. This tool enables Kidsgrove to predict the performance of all processes: preparation, assembly and even final delivery, before production has actually begun. The quality model also permits analysis of 'what if' scenarios, so that quality decisions can be taken at the design stage (see Figure 4.8), and it therefore underpins the Taguchi design system mentioned above.

Another development in quality monitoring has been the introduction of machine capability measurement. The continuing thrust is away from control and towards the prevention of non-conformance. All responsibility for inspection has been devolved down to the individuals who control production processes. Only two inspection stages now remain at the Kidsgrove site: one at the final stage of bare board production, and the other when boards have been assembled and tested (a visual check), which is part of the packing, labelling and dispatch process.

As the pace of change increases, the Kidsgrove operation foresees an increasing need to focus the activities of QCs and CATs. The system of focused facilitation currently being developed will preferentially encourage CATs and QCs whose projects impact on the key macro-processes which drive the business. This aspect of the QIP is supported by various personnel initiatives. For example, free private medical care has recently been introduced for all employees, and a parallel, free counselling service to promote staff welfare.

Philip Crosby insists that the quality process should never end, otherwise: 'there is a great sigh of relief when goals are reached. If you are not careful, the entire program will end at that moment' (Crosby, 1979, p. 257). No. 14 of Crosby's steps is 'Do it over again', so a study of a successful quality improvement process can only ever be a snapshot of a moment in the life of that process. This chapter has examined the factors which made the process necessary as well as the decisions, actions and systems which have made it work. There is another Crosby-ism which goes: 'You have to lead people gently toward what they already know is right' (Crosby, 1979, p. 129). That is definitely ICL's experience. The need for cultural change and devolvement of responsibility was recognized by management as early as 1983. Their subsequent realization has been the mechanism and driving force of the QIP. They are basic ingredients of strategy and policy now being made, which will carry the company forward into the future.

GLOSSARY OF ABBREVIATIONS

BABT   British Approvals Board Telephones: accrediting body for telephone systems electronics.

CA Corrective action: the second stage of the corrective action process, instigated when the ECR fails to provide a solution because of the problem size or difficulty.

CAR Corrective action report: management reporting system for CA.

CAT Corrective action team: small group, usually of experts, chosen by management to solve a specific problem.

CBL Computer-based learning: educational software applications which allow individuals to learn, practise and self-assess skills without input from a teacher.

ECR Error cause removal: first stage of a system for identifying and removing the problems noted by employees.

ICL International Computers Ltd: the parent company.

JIT Just-in-time: system of keeping inventory to a minimum by minimizing ordering and holding times.

KMO Kidsgrove Manufacturing Operation: printed circuit board manufacturing operation at the ICL Kidsgrove plant.

KZDD Kidsgrove Zero Defects Day: 12 September 1990, the day set aside at the Kidsgrove site for public declarations of the zero defects philosophy by management and workers.

NSQT National Society for Quality through Teamwork: group of industrialists which sponsors quality awards and forums.

PCA Printed circuit assembly: department of KMO.

PMS Product and material supply: department of KMO.

PONC Price of non-conformance: the cost of getting it wrong.

PPC Printed circuit fabrication: department of KMO.

QAG Quality action group: departmental or area team set up on a more or less informal basis by a supervisor/manager.

QC Quality circle: group of employees who meet voluntarily in work time to identify and solve quality problems affecting their work.

QCSC Quality circle steering committee: team at Kidsgrove works level, set up to steer and monitor the activities of QCs.

QIFTI Quality improvement for the individual: ICL's first series of in-house training courses on quality.

QIP Quality improvement process: the whole programme of quality development, company-wide.

QIST Quality improvement steering team: team at ICL divisional level set up to steer and monitor the activities of site QITs.

QIT Quality improvement team: committee consisting of site managers plus stepholders responsible for individual quality steps. Meets monthly to coordinate the QIP.

Area QIT Area quality improvement team: departmental version of quality improvement team.

SPC Statistical process control.

TLA Three-letter abbreviation: tongue-in-cheek way of describing the jargon of acronyms surrounding the QIP.

TTT Tools, techniques and teamwork: problem-solving course for ICL employees.

ZD Zero defects: the ethos that employees should always strive to eliminate all defects.

REFERENCES

Crosby, P. B. (1979) *Quality Is Free: The Art of Making Quality Certain*, McGraw-Hill, New York.

Crosby, P. B. (1984) *Quality Without Tears: The Art of Hassle-Free Management*, McGraw-Hill, New York.

Lorenz, C. (1986) 'A painful process of change', *Financial Times*, 14 May, pp. 6–7.

Moralee, D. (1981) 'The ICL story', *Electronics and Power*, vol. 27, no. 11, pp. 788–95. This provides a more detailed account of ICL's history to 1981.

Oakland, J. S. (1989) *Total Quality Management*, Butterworth/Heinemann, London, pp. 185–6.

FIVE

LAND ROVER:
Extraordinary customer satisfaction
– the road to success

TONY INGOLD
AND
TREVOR WORTHINGTON

FIVE

Land Rover:

Extraordinary customer satisfaction – the road to success

INTRODUCTION

The Rover Group is Britain's largest motor manufacturer, producing half a million vehicles a year. The group designs, manufactures and markets cars in the small, medium and executive sectors, and car-derived vans and specialist four-wheel-drive vehicles. As a subsidiary of British Aerospace, it is now part of Britain's largest manufacturing and engineering organization and one of Europe's largest companies. The Rover Group, with annual sales of £3,700 million and exports of over £1,100 million, is the UK's leading car producer and exporter, selling its vehicles in 150 markets worldwide.

Land Rover is the marque name for the company's world-famous four-wheel-drive vehicles – the Defender, Discovery and Range Rover – manufactured at Solihull. About 8,000 people are employed at the highly integrated Lode Lane site, designing, manufacturing and assembling engines, gearboxes, axles and bodies, painting, trimming and finally assembling the complete vehicle. Land Rover is fully committed to becoming a total quality company and being internationally renowned for extraordinary customer satisfaction.

In the early 1980s the combined sales of Land Rover and Range Rover fell to an unprecedented low of 35,000 units in the face of new emerging products in the 4 × 4 sector. The competition was led primarily by Japanese manufacturers in the form of Toyota, Isuzu and Daihatsu. Initial examples did not match the off-road capability of the Land Rover products. However, they did provide value-for-money alternatives to a new customer body who did not necessarily demand such basic off-road prowess. Land Rover had hitherto been unrivalled in the 4 × 4 market, and had enjoyed an unchallenged period during which a full order book was the norm and the pace of product change was largely drawn from within the business. The competition rapidly evolved their products from those initially presented, and by the mid to late 1980s had established a significant foothold in the traditional 4 × 4 sector. Furthermore, the competition also tapped into a new rich vein of 4 × 4 customers in the passenger/

leisure sector. New levels of product quality and reliability shortened product development cycles, and high levels of specification stengthened the Japanese market position and took customer expectations to new levels.

Faced with growing competitive pressures and diminishing market share, Land Rover had to refocus the business in terms of both understanding customer expectations and satisfying these through cultural change. The business had a traditional function-based organization which precipitated poor communication across departments and engendered instances of an isolated approach to meeting customer requirements. In addition, there was still an autocratic and somewhat adversarial management style, which was a legacy of the British motor industry. This chapter explains how these challenges were addressed.

LAND ROVER

The Land Rover company has had varying fortunes over its history. Land Rover vehicles were almost a product of serendipity and arose as a result of the austerity measures following the Second World War. The Rover company, which was the innovator of the Land Rover vehicle, began by producing sewing machines in the 1860s. This business developed to produce bicycles, then motorcycles and finally cars. The company built its foundation on quality cars, but this did not protect it from the problems posed by the recession of the 1930s. However, history shows that the company survived. The old Rover works were bombed in 1940 and the company obtained two new sites, one of which was in Solihull, the site of the present Land Rover factory (see Figure 5.1).

Following the Second World War, there was a general shortage of steel, and the Rover company was restricted in the number of vehicles it was allowed to produce by the government. It was at this point that innovators within the company realized that there was a market niche for a versatile farm utility vehicle, the design of which was based on the Jeep of the Second World War.

The new vehicle underwent a rapid development programme and used many components from the pre-war Rover cars. The decision to build a new 'vehicle for the land' based loosely around the four-wheel-drive Willys Jeep was taken in the spring of 1947. The first vehicle was shown to the public in April 1948 at the Amsterdam Motor Show.

The vehicle was innovative in several ways, the innovations being forced by low budget and steel shortage. Perhaps the most interesting feature was the use of aluminium alloy for all the body panels. This meant that new methods of body panel production had to be used with minimal cost in press tools. A second innovation for this type of vehicle was the use of a relatively small engine. A third innovation was the design of multiple power take-off points, allowing the vehicle to be used as a farm utility. The final product was a cheap and versatile utility vehicle which was rapidly accepted by the public, farmers and, not originally planned for, military applications. At this early stage, every Land Rover built was rapidly purchased.

During the 1950s the vehicle underwent a steady development process and gained worldwide fame for its endurance. In 1970 an innovative step was the introduction of a new luxury four-wheel-drive vehicle, the Range Rover. In the following years the Range Rover was gradually developed into the superior luxury car that we see today.

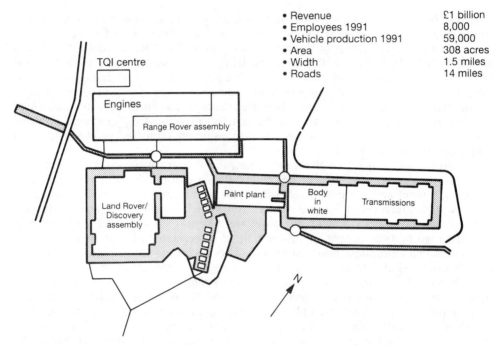

• Revenue	£1 billion
• Employees 1991	8,000
• Vehicle production 1991	59,000
• Area	308 acres
• Width	1.5 miles
• Roads	14 miles

Figure 5.1 Land Rover business

However, despite this history of innovation, market research showed that customers did not want radical changes to the external appearance of the vehicles. Worldwide sales of both vehicles continued to increase and the company still commanded a strong market position. This strong market position was undoubtedly in part the result of a lack of competition, but this situation was set to change with the entry of the Japanese manufacturers into the four-wheel-drive market and, to a lesser extent, with the new and severe United States vehicle emission regulations, which were rigorously enforced.

The Japanese effectively created a new passenger/leisure market sector. To compete in this sector the company produced a new product, the Discovery, which was launched in 1989. This vehicle is now the most successful in the leisure sector. In 1992 the vehicle commanded 37 per cent of this market, while its nearest rival held only 20 per cent market share.

Over the years, the company also had to contend with a range of internal and external political interferences and changes of management and ownership, which must have created serious instability. For many years, Land Rover existed as a division of Rover cars, but in 1978 it became a company in its own right, albeit under the wing of British Leyland. Before this, from the late 1960s the company had been hampered by undercapitalization at a time of opportunity, with a weak pound and a growing demand for four-wheel-drive vehicles. With the appointment of a new chairman in 1978, a large-scale shake-up of the management was carried out and a major investment programme undertaken. Unfortunately, the company did not pay enough attention to marketing or to dealer education for customer service.

The company still maintained its developed and traditional base of military sales, both at home and overseas, probably because of the robust build and longevity of its vehicles. Indeed, the latter quality may well prove a vital competitive edge in the future when the steel-bodied Japanese vehicles purchased earlier have to be replaced.

Prior to the introduction of a total quality policy, Land Rover had a traditional British industrial policy, including the clear delineation of worker roles, the inspection of components from suppliers and the subsequent rejection of faulty or out-of-tolerance components; faulty products and customer complaints were treated on a 'dealer will put it right' basis. All of these were accepted as normal practice, although senior executives at Land Rover were beginning to realize, from evidence gathered from other manufacturers, that customers considered fault-free products to be a major criterion for satisfaction.

Unfortunately, at this time the trade unions saw the recent success of the company as a major opportunity for a large pay claim. Because of the differing perceptions of the management and the unions as to the state of the company, a strike was called early in 1988 which lasted for five weeks. New vehicle development and production were continued by management, the gates were kept open and there was a gradual return to work. One benefit of this period of disruption was that there arose an awareness that communication had previously been too much of a one-way process and that steps needed to be taken to develop two-way communications.

Following the return to work the company promoted a quality awareness programme by introducing a quality link campaign and discussion groups (quality circles), and by placing an increased emphasis on its suggestion scheme. A consultant was engaged to provide training and motivation for the discussion groups. The result of the foregoing was the introduction in 1989 of a total quality improvement (TQI) programme which focused on customer satisfaction and was 'management led', empowering employees and developing democratic management. The Perkins Award, on which this chapter is based, was a study of the changes taking place in Land Rover from March 1991 to March 1992. It is awarded to the company demonstrating the greatest commitment to a programme of total involvement in quality.

The sections which follow address a number of facets of Land Rover's quality improvement programme:

- Quality improvement strategy and mission policy.
- Integration into day-to-day operations.
- Land Rover training.
- Quality measurements.
- Management commitment.

QUALITY IMPROVEMENT STRATEGY AND MISSION POLICY

The Rover Group vision aims to ensure that 'Rover is internationally renowned for extraordinary customer satisfaction.' The quality strategy was developed by the Rover Group board to support the company. In January 1991, Rover Group reorganized its operations into product supply business units. At Solihull, three units were established, each with its own managing director:

- Land Rover Vehicles.
- Land Rover Powertrain.
- Land Rover Commercial.

Within the overall strategy, each business unit developed its implementation plans to suit its own particular requirements, together with its mission statement and objectives. Mission statements have also been developed at function level to confirm their commitment to the overall company vision.

The development of the organization over the past 12 months has refined the management's commitment, energy, enthusiasm and determination to manage the company in line with the philosophy of total quality. A key output has been the production of a five-year quality strategy.

INTEGRATION INTO DAY-TO-DAY OPERATIONS

This section provides a comprehensive review of the actions taken by the two manufacturing business units, Land Rover Vehicles and Land Rover Powertrain, at Solihull in order to support the strategic initiatives and objectives for 1991 onwards. The main focus was identified as cost reduction and quality improvement through the following:

- Processes: reduce defects and cycle time.
- People: participation and empowerment.

Processes

The step changes which took place during 1991 have been possible only as a result of the cultural and attitudinal changes brought about by the total quality initiative. This has facilitated a number of developments:

- Clarity of objectives.
- The establishment of milestone measurements.
- The development of teamwork through functional management teams and by the introduction of cell management. This has focused accountability for quality of output closer to the workplace and has produced a streamlined and effective management structure.

During 1991 the 1,200-mile audit, now called the finished vehicle audit, was the key measure of quality. (A description of the audit is given later.) This was communicated to all employees weekly, in support of the company mission.

Within the Land Rover Vehicle business unit, the managing director and his first line manager each championed a breakthrough project. These projects were selected to address major quality concerns raised through the audit and often required a review of design and manufacturing processes. The projects were all broad-based and often required involvement, help and assistance from all functional areas. Measurement and review on a regular basis are key features of the management of projects.

The need to introduce effective measurement of the processes within manufacturing was really taken to heart during 1991. As an example, Powertrain developed further its total preventive maintenance programme (TPM). This moved from the reactive role of 'when it breaks fix it' to a proactive role of prevention – examining every machine, identifying any faults or possible future failure areas and taking action.

Figure 5.2 shows a challenging plan, set at the start of 1991, to review every machine the company had in its manufacturing areas. The target figures were exceeded, as shown by the diagram for North Works.

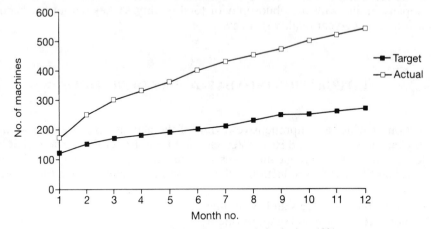

Figure 5.2   North Works clean and check plan, 1991

Having introduced the TPM programme, statistical process control (SPC) can then be meaningfully applied, and 1991 saw a dramatic increase in the number of components and attributes being controlled. (A more detailed explanation is given later.)

People

Throughout 1991 and into 1992, Land Rover continued with total quality improvement (TQI) training to ensure that the philosophy was taken to everyone in the company. This enabled the cultural changes required progressively to become a natural part of day-to-day activities. The programme focuses on the following aspects:

- Teamworking within and across all functions.
- Internal and external customer satisfaction.
- Process improvement and the elimination of waste in all functions.
- Investment in prevention.
- Management leadership.

When the total quality programme began in 1989, considerable efforts were made to ensure that this was not seen as 'just another initiative'. The dedicated TQI centre, built at a cost of £100,000, had an extra training room added in 1990 to support the company's needs and the building was used daily throughout 1991 either for TQI training or in support of other activities:

- Performance management training.
- Quality action teams training.

- Total customer satisfaction training (a programme for the commercial business unit to deliver to the dealer organization).
- Discussion groups.
- Quality council meetings.
- Business awareness seminars.

Teams: structure and function

Of key importance in achieving Land Rover's quality improvement objectives was the evolution of a variety of teams, with various structures and functions, that would facilitate an improvement in communication and the removal of barriers between managers and associates.

Team structures

At the beginning of 1991 a radical restructuring of the company and the introduction of business units was undertaken in order to develop a closer team environment and to focus even closer attention on product delivery at the best possible quality level. This also provided the opportunity for fully implementing the cell management concept, which had been under development during 1990. Cell management has greatly assisted the increase in teamwork, involving cell managers, facilitators, team leaders and conformance engineers. Figure 5.3 shows a typical example of a cell structure.

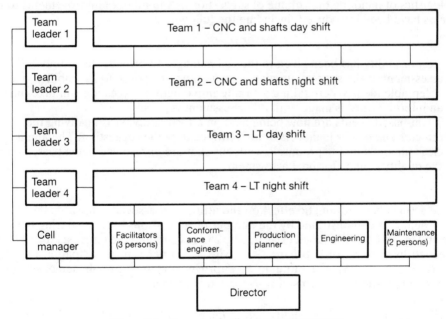

Figure 5.3   Example of cell management structure

Obstacles

Some initial reservations from trade unions were addressed through full consultation.

The introduction of a number of new roles, particularly team leaders, necessitated the implementation of new and comprehensive training programmes.

Methods of problem identification and correction

The finished vehicle audit provides one of the main measurement indicators for the movement towards the vision of extraordinary customer satisfaction. This involves a detailed customer perspective audit based on a random selection of finished vehicles. Considerable progress was made during 1991, and the challenging quality targets for all vehicles were met by the year end. These targets have now been adjusted to an even more demanding level for 1992 and 1993.

At local level, right first time (RFT) is the main measure, with daily briefings held at the end of shift to communicate the causes of problems experienced that day and to review action taken.

Encouragement of innovation

Suggestion schemes   During 1991 the need to extend the empowerment of associates (employees) so as to improve the vehicle and working conditions was linked to review and constant revision, with considerable concentration placed on the development of the suggestion scheme, which was called 'Bright I's'.

The success achieved through the increasing growth of the scheme placed strains on the logistics of handling the volume of suggestions. A number of improvements to the process have been introduced, including the following:

- Responsibility has been given to the cell manager to provide the initial assessment of the suggestion, giving a very quick response to its viability as an acceptable idea. Where taking action to implement a suggestion will take time, an interim award is made until full assessment is possible.
- Team-based events are now being held on a fortnightly basis involving the director and senior managers of areas affected by the suggestion. The aim is to clear the outstanding proposals, with any that are unresolved being passed on to the quality council for final assessment.

These actions had a dramatic effect on the attitude of associates towards the suggestion scheme, as demonstrated by the number of suggestions received during the year. The end of 1991 saw the target exceeded by 25 per cent, and the target set for 1992 was exceeded by the end of February 1992, with a 200 per cent participation rate. The quality of suggestions is continuing to improve, and this growth demonstrates an encouraging response in terms of workforce involvement.

Quality action teams   The quality action team (QAT) is a multidisciplined team of relevant fact holders who come together voluntarily for the purpose of resolving a product quality-related problem. It will have a 'sponsor' from the product area involved, who will provide any necessary 'coaching' to team members from other areas to support the work of the QAT, and will identify to whom the result will be presented. Typically, a QAT will have six to eight members who come from varying levels within the organization and are nominated to join the QAT by their managers. QATs meet at least weekly, if necessary outside normal working hours, and the team disbands once the problem has been resolved. There are six stages to the QAT process, as shown in Figure 5.4.

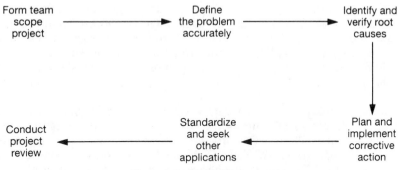

Figure 5.4 The QAT process

The methodology of QATs is quite complex and the disciplined structure requires training for QAT leaders. The QAT structure is explained to managers through a briefing sheet. As the numbers of QATs increased across the site during 1991, there was a need to appoint local coordinators to oversee local QAT processes. It is important that the establishment of QATs is controlled by the sponsors because there is a danger that many members of a department could be involved in a number of QATs at any one time. This would obviously be to the detriment of the parent department's performance.

There are, in many instances, cross-functional and group-wide QATs which have been used to resolve some very difficult problems which had previously been considered unresolvable. At local level, where the scope is far less complex, some very worthwhile results have been achieved. The success and value of QATs to the business has influenced the structure of the next phase of TQI training. This was developed through 1991, with over 107 managers, facilitators and team leaders being trained in delivering it. The number of QATs increased from 85 in 1990, to 214 in 1991, and to 370 in 1992.

Discussion groups A discussion group programme was introduced to Land Rover during the early part of 1988. This programme is Land Rover's equivalent to quality circles. The groups' brief has not changed significantly since the inception of the programme and is characterized as follows:

• Approximately six people from the same or similar work area meet to solve a variety of work-related problems on a long-term basis.
• They identify their own work-related problems.
• They decide which problem(s) to investigate at any one time.
• They investigate problem(s) using data-gathering methods and problem analysis techniques.

- They discuss potential solutions to problems, involving relevant 'fact holders' when necessary.
- They gain the necessary authority for solutions to be implemented.
- They either ensure that the solution is put in place or carry out the solution as a discussion group.

Guidelines as to 'acceptable' problems for discussion groups to investigate are as unrestrictive as possible. Groups are asked to focus on work-related problems, but these can include anything from the quality of product and process to environmental issues. The only constraints placed on the groups are that they should not investigate terms and conditions of employment. Nine groups were established during the first year of the programme. Since this time, the groups have gone from strength to strength.

The number of groups grew significantly in 1991 from 45 to 66, an increase of over 50 per cent. The interesting feature of the growth experienced during the second part of the year was that much of it was driven by individuals making it known that they wanted to be part of a group. As well as individual groups proving themselves in their own areas, the increased exposure given to groups through *Land Rover News* played a significant part. For the company this was an encouraging sign, as the objective has always been for groups to be 'self-driven'.

In 1992 there were 804 discussion groups in operation, a massive increase over a period of only four years. By the end of 1991 there were 468 people involved in a discussion group (figures for persons involved in 1992 are not yet available), which equates to the involvement of approximately 6 per cent of associates.

The success of the discussion groups programme is a direct result of the considerable support it is afforded by the company. This includes time for group members to hold regular weekly meetings and for training and presentations. A permanent discussion group coordinator and facilitator are employed. They are responsible for promoting the programme, encouraging new growth, facilitating new groups' initial start-up period and maintaining and supporting existing groups.

The managing directors of Land Rover Vehicles and Powertrain respectively clearly demonstrate their support by reading every set of minutes produced by the groups on site. They often comment personally on a problem, and make the effort to see as many groups as possible in action. On a practical level, it is through the managing directors' encouragement that their managers continue supporting the groups.

As the number of discussion groups has grown, the agendas of the mature groups have moved away from the working environment to concentrate on quality of product and process improvement. Discussion groups frequently report their successes to Rover board members at the quarterly business unit reviews, and an annual event is held to recognize all the groups' efforts. It has taken a lot of hard work and dedication, but the results are now speaking for themselves: over 500 problems were solved in 1992.

Performance management (PM) scheme   During 1991 a pilot scheme was developed within the Powertrain transmissions function. It is a data-based system for managing human performance. Desired results were determined, and behaviours which would accomplish these were pinpointed. Progress towards results was then measured in order to determine when to give positive reinforcement for continued improvement.

The principle is that negative reinforcement will only encourage people to do just enough, whereas positive reinforcement will draw performance out of people – in particular, the additional discretionary level of performance which supports continuous improvement.

While still in its early stages, the pilot scheme was received extremely well and has, from the performance management matrices developed so far, pinpointed areas for improvement. Details of areas that have improved as a result of the PM scheme are discussed later.

Learning from failure

As a result of TQI and the theme of continuous improvement, the word 'failure' has been replaced by 'opportunity', and the company tries to emphasize to all its employees that they can view all problems as an opportunity to learn.

One of the best examples of learning from failure is the introduction of statistical process control (SPC). Originally implemented as an initiative in 1988, it was driven by a target and deadline – x attributes have to be measured by y date. It was achieved, but soon fell into disrepute, mainly because the company did not act on the results and still had an inspection system to control the process. In 1991 it took another look at how it could reintroduce SPC and make it work.

Land Rover's previous experience indicated that part of the cause of the failure of SPC was that management did not understand the process or what it could achieve. The company also had to take action and carry out capability studies on the machines first to ensure that the SPC measurement was meaningful. It relaunched SPC coupled with performance management in the transmissions area and this, together with the TPM programme, has enabled the operators to take control of their own process. The following predicted benefits of SPC have been identified:

- It gives operator control of quality.
- It is not dependent on end-of-line inspection.
- It reduces the need for separate inspection functions.
- It enables measurement of capability/repeatability of the process.
- It will indicate deterioration in the process before defects are produced, thus facilitating a TPM.
- By assisting TPM, less downtime and hence more components are produced, and capacity is increased.
- Because the condition of the process is known, predictable and more reliable just-in-time production becomes feasible.
- It highlights incapable processes and provides a date for machine replacement.
- It provides a record of process improvement which indicates when an action improves the process.
- If machined components are controlled around nominal size, assembly fit is more consistent and predictable, and the need for selective assembly is reduced.
- It provides a common language between operators, shifts, maintenance, engineering and other roles.
- It indicates process disturbance, e.g. machine start-up/stop, temperature variation, tool changes, raw material changes.
- It gives visible proof of quality of process.
- It reduces the cost of production associated with rework and scrap.

LAND ROVER TRAINING

Uniquely within British industry, a separate company, the Rover Learning Business (RLB), has been created to ensure a concentrated focus on training for all people within Rover. More numerous and more easily accessible training opportunities have been developed, including a scheme for non-job-related training for all employees. The RLB complements the site training departments – the relationship is one of close partnership and the structure and function are set out below.

Land Rover training – internal

It is strongly felt within Land Rover that all training on offer can be viewed as quality improvement training. Whether it be on-the-job instruction, off-the-job theoretical training or an evening non-vocational course, training conveys the message to Land Rover employees that they are an important part of the business. All the training given to employees enables them to make an improved contribution, whether by increasing their skill level, their appreciation of new techniques or their feeling of self-worth.

The training department provides a range of facilities and utilizes on-the-job situations and off-site facilities in order to ensure that all courses are delivered in the most appropriate manner. It also has a dedicated training staff, all experts in their own field, who deliver training and develop new courses to meet the changing demands of the business and of its people.

The training department had some 147 courses available during 1991. It is possible to split these courses into three main types: (a) individual open-learning packages, (b) group 'off-the-job' manual skill-focused training and (c) group 'off-the-job office/supervisory/managerial-focused training, as set out below.

Individual open learning

There is an employee development centre (EDC) at Land Rover which provides a facility for individual learning and development for any employee. The majority of the 86 courses provided at the EDC are computer based, although there are also audio and video learning packages available. The training department produces an EDC course brochure so that individuals can choose the course they wish to study. The principle of the centre is that every individual is responsible for his or her own learning, and all courses are designed to meet this aim. However, there is a full-time member of the training department on hand to offer help if it is required.

Employees can undertake courses which are either job related or purely of personal interest. Generally, when a course is job related, people can study in the EDC during working hours. If a course is non-vocational, bookings can be made outside working hours. The EDC is open from 8.00 a.m. to 7.30 p.m. from Monday to Thursday, and normal office hours (8.00 a.m. to 4.10 p.m.) on Friday. No charge is made for any courses undertaken in the EDC. This type of learning has proved to be very popular within Land Rover and the level of demand for EDC courses is constant.

Off-the-job training

During 1991, the Land Rover training department offered 63 types of in-house course which were run 'off-the-job' in Land Rover's own facilities. Supplementing these were courses run by external bodies on Land Rover's behalf either on the company's premises or on their own. Courses are publicized throughout the site by way of a training opportunities brochure which clearly makes the point that, if a course does not exist already, the training department may be able to provide a suitable course.

During 1991, Land Rover spent £7 million on off-the-job training. This equates to just under £1,000 per head per annum. This is a significant financial investment in employees and further demonstrates the commitment to training during the year. The courses described below are key example of the training philosophy in action.

Supervisory/managerial-focused training

Team leader training The team leader, as previously mentioned, is a key member of the cell management structure which is now in operation. Team leaders are responsible, within each cell, for quality aspects and training of team members. Each team leader selected during 1991 went through an intensive two-week off-the-job training period before he or she was put into the new position. The training course covered basic issues such as how to train people, an introduction to company processes and procedures, person management skills and an important focus on quality.

While fully expecting the training to harness the commitment of the new team leaders to get involved with company aims, it also brought unexpected benefits. Throughout 1991, team leader training appears to have had a significant impact on the quality of Land Rover products. Results of 1,200-mile audits improved steadily throughout the year. By explaining the issues surrounding quality to the team leaders and then empowering them to improve the quality of work done within their teams, the company has succeeded in moving a step closer to both its quality and involvement aims.

Statistical process control (SPC) In 1991 Land Rover began to place much greater emphasis on the use of SPC. It was therefore very important that it had a structured training course which would highlight to people what SPC was and how it could be used effectively. The training allowed Land Rover Powertrain to implement SPC in a controlled and useful manner. By careful and considered introduction after training, it found that people at all levels understood what SPC did and why it was necessary. Significant quality savings have arisen as a result of this.

Integrated management development scheme (IMDS) This programme was developed in conjunction with Warwick University and is a notable example of training commissioned by Land Rover, but provided by an external body. The target population for IMDS is production managers. Its objective is to provide training and development in basic business techniques, quality techniques and systems, which is intended to supplement and enhance the managers' production knowledge. Forty managers took part in IMDS during 1991, the objective being that every production manager will eventually go through the scheme.

Training by outside agencies

The training department has a crucial role to play in the training of employees. However, during 1991, the company aimed to reinforce the message that there are external agencies and experts who are more suitable providers of certain training.

Three examples of training provided from outside the training department umbrella are total quality improvement (TQI), discussion group, and performance management training.

Total quality improvement training   The programme of TQI training which commenced in 1988 with the directors, executives and managers gradually cascaded down through the organization in line with the TQI programme (Figure 5.5).

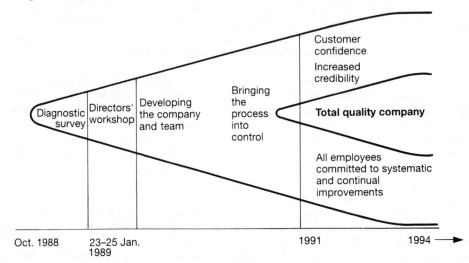

Figure 5.5   The TQI programme

In order to reinforce the commitment of TQI and develop the team, delivery to the associates has been by their own management and facilitators, these having been trained in both facilitating skills and the course material. Key managers from each function developed the course material to meet specific needs following a survey to identify the core requirements.

The TQI programme has been developed around seven basic principles:

- The philosophy – prevention not detection.
- The approach – management led.
- The scale – everyone responsible (commitment).
- The measure – cost of quality.
- The standard – right first time.
- The scope – company-wide (touches everybody).
- The theme – continuous improvement.

On completion of the course, all participants receive a certificate, lapel pin and a handbook. The handbook emphasizes the key themes which form the core understanding. These are all the requirements needed to ensure that the company moves forward to achieve its ultimate vision.

The themes are as follows:

- Everyone has customers and suppliers. The understanding of this has been one of the most significant changes in the company attitude.

- People make quality. This is reinforced by the change in people's attitude and their participation in suggestion schemes; a prime example of workforce-driven innovation.
- Teamwork. The increases in discussion groups and quality action teams are prime examples of what can be achieved through teams working together.
- Communication. Land Rover has made great strides through the introduction of Team Brief, Scene (an electronic notice board system installed across the site in amenity areas) and other forms of internal communication.
- Prevention. The change in attitude towards right first time and the emphasis on ownership/empowerment has enabled the position of inspection to become redundant.

Apart from a few people who missed their training through illness or shift changes, the first phase of TQI was completed with 6,000 employees being trained in 1992.

Performance management training   Performance management was piloted in the Transmissions area. The concept and initial training took place through an external consultancy, Baker Davis. All management went through four half-days of training, split over four weeks, together with 10 two-hour follow-up sessions with the consultant. The results were demonstrated through detailed measurements.

Discussion group training   During 1991, great emphasis was placed on giving discussion group members useful training in order to increase their performance and give the groups greater structure. The discussion group coordinator or facilitator gave every new group a structured initial training of two hours per week for a period of six weeks. Also, every individual who joined an established group was supported for the initial two sessions by one of the discussion group facilitation team – this in addition to the support offered by the longer-serving members of the group themselves.

Land Rover also continued the ambitious programme of dedicated off-site training aimed at all discussion group members of over six months' membership. The format is a two-day session aimed at introducing/reinforcing some basic problem-solving and teamwork concepts. The delegates for each training session were chosen with a view to allowing discussion group members from a variety of areas to mix, share experiences and benefit from each other's ideas.

An obvious need for further training of longer-serving discussion group members was identified in 1991. To this end, the company ran a pilot course towards the end of 1991 aimed at those people who had been discussion group members for over two years. Again, a two-day off-site course; this time the objective was to introduce some more complex problem-solving techniques and to refresh people's minds about techniques they had learned some time ago. The feedback from the delegates was very positive and, as a result, the company is running two further sessions during 1992 to include more of the longer-serving members. Both two-day courses were run by an external consultant at an off-site location – factors which reinforce the importance of the training to the delegates.

The scale of the commitment to discussion group training is illustrated by the fact that a total of 4,784 hours of training were provided. By the end of 1991 the discussion group members had received approximately 10 hours of training per member during the year.

External customers and suppliers

The training of dealers and suppliers has been undertaken by the commercial business unit with respect to the dealers, and by the group purchasing unit regarding Land Rover's suppliers. Towards the end of 1991, at the request of suppliers, the Power-train business unit started to provide SPC training, and this was extended through 1992.

QUALITY MEASUREMENTS

Quality measurements at Land Rover are based on a number of criteria of which the following are important, and will be described here:

- Finished product.
- Processes.
- People.

It is considered that any process improvement, whether it be within manufacturing or the service function, has its part to play in the overall improvement of the company, and in its endeavour to become recognized for providing extraordinary customer satisfaction. The total company's organization measurement system is based on the critical success factor concept.

Finished product

As mentioned previously, the key measurement system for vehicle quality improve-ment is the finished vehicle audit. The finished vehicle audit undertaken by central quality audit (independent evaluation) tests 10 vehicles per week. Its report is avail-able at the audit stations immediately on completion of the audit. On a daily basis the directors and managers visit the audit area to see the problems identified, and then return to their respective functions to take steps to correct where appropriate. Where possible, operators are invited to the audit area to see the problem for themselves.

While there is an overall vehicle demerit, the causes are broken down to function, i.e. paint, vehicle assembly, engines, transmissions. These measurements are char-tered and provide both upper and lower control limits and the mean achieved over the week/month.

Using the same system of demerits, each major unit function has its own audits, e.g. engine strip, gearbox, axle, paint. Both problems and successes are reported back to line management and the operators.

The breakthrough projects, identified earlier, were established to address problems which required a review of the design and manufacturing processes. Significant im-provements have been achieved on the Discovery model: the overall reduction in demerits between August and December 1991 (the period in which the project ran) can be used to illustrate this. A target of 35 or fewer demerits per month was set and a level of 25 was achieved. The processes involved may be exemplified by those used in the Powertrain business unit as set out below.

Powertrain quality measures and failure rectification

Measurement and frequency

- *Finished vehicle audit*   All Powertrain defects detected during the internal customer appraisal are separately reported and reviewed weekly by the Powertrain managing director.
- *Black box*   Any Powertrain defect detected during vehicle build and/or rolling road pass-off is recorded daily and reported back to the appropriate major unit cell (e.g. transfer box) for team briefing. This is reviewed weekly by the managing director (100 per cent sampling).
- *Right first time*   All cases of build away from process (misfit) or test reject are recorded daily and the score summarized as a per cent RFT for report back into the assembly cell. Again, this is reviewed weekly by the managing director (100 per cent sampling).
- *Strip audit*   Sample batches (usually four) of major units are stripped, measured and examined. This audit will detect 'out of specification' items which could pass black box and finished vehicle audit, but may cause customer complaint during the life of the vehicle (reviewed weekly).

Prevention – by problem   All defects, wherever detected, are automatically rectified. However, no problem is closed until the failure mode is fully diagnosed and design or process revision undergoes trial on track. Each problem has an owner and progress is measured weekly by the managing directors.

Prevention – general   During 1991 a total prevention project began with the aim of putting quality improvement in the hands of the associates. This is driven by a discussion group with production associate, audit staff, production management and engineering and logistics members. This systematic approach has sponsored several major activities:

- Process audit by operator interview.
- Teaming engineers with cell activities.
- Product awareness training for all manufacturing managers and eventually team leaders.
- Exchange visits with local companies/suppliers selected because of their excellent teamwork.
- A direct supplier quality link.
- Visits to dealers to understand service failure modes.

Processes

The process is measured by right first time (RFT) achievement throughout manufacturing and assembly. Land Rover has a system of 'buy off' between cells, which is the point at which that part of the process should be complete and any problems which have been identified should have been corrected. These achievements are documented and form part of the daily/weekly management review.

Within the machining areas, SPC is becoming the main measurement system for controlling the process. For example, the following activities are measured:

- The critical feature control plan for both Land Rover components and Rover car components (Land Rover manufactures and assembles the front suspension for the Metro).
- Cell details relating to the component, the machine, the feature being controlled, the type of chart, the control plan index and the problems being experienced.
- The planned introduction of SPC activities for both Land Rover and Rover products.

One example of RFT measure is shown in Figure 5.6.

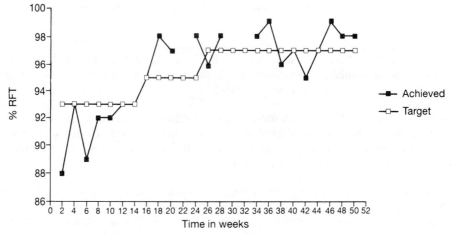

Figure 5.6   V8 engine test: per cent right first time (RFT)

People

The achievement of total quality can come only from a change in attitude of the workforce. The step change which has to be achieved is the breaking down of barriers – the 'them and us' syndrome.

Land Rover has put a lot of effort into the TQI programme and into cultivating a management attitude change. Before commencing phase 2 of the TQI programme, each function is carrying out a survey of its associates. The indications are that the company is moving in the right direction.

When managing the performance of people there is a need to pinpoint the key variables in an individual's job. They should be variables over which that individual has control. There is then a need to measure performance against each of these variables, for which a performance matrix is used. A performance manager has been appointed who not only produces the statistics but also coaches the managers. The key variables identified are as follows:

- RFT.
- Output.
- Off standards.
- Overtime.
- Scrap.
- Absence.

All of these play an important part in the achievement of the critical success factors. While only fully operational since the last quarter of 1991, this system has already produced significant changes.

An important aspect of PM is that the manager is very reliant on the support of his or her team in the improvement of performance, and this is having an effect on workplace attitudes. In essence, people are now more supportive, and this is encouraging synergystic working between managers and associates.

MANAGEMENT COMMITMENT

Demonstrating management commitment to quality improvement

The introduction of TQM/TQI has changed the organization so dramatically over the past three years that it becomes difficult to describe an approach which has gradually become a way of life within the company. Commitment to quality improvement is taken as giving 100 per cent, and demonstrating this commitment is one of the company's key focal points.

Each Land Rover business unit has a quality council which is composed of the managing director and his first line of managers. The objectives set by the quality council of the Land Rover vehicles business unit clearly identify the commitment to quality improvement, with a measurement structure to enable constant monitoring and review.

In turn, each of the business unit functions has its own quality steering group, membership consisting of the function director and his first line of management, and representation from other functions and associates as required. As the quality steering groups become established, there are proposals for them to be set up at local management level. Management commitment is also demonstrated in a number of other ways:

- The increased support being given to the associates in releasing them from their normal work in order to participate in discussion groups and training.
- Attendance at discussion group/providing support when requested.
- Sponsorship of QATs, which requires not only the release of their own associates to resolve their concerns, but also assisting other managers in resolving their problems. This applies equally to improvement groups.
- Team briefs which occur across the company, with production stopping for around 20 minutes weekly to enable production managers, facilitators and team

leaders to carry out the briefings. Where there is a two- or three-shift pattern operating, there is also a daily shift briefing to communicate problems and actions taken during the previous shift.

- The work and effort being applied to introduce the single-status company.
- The continued development of the TQI centre and the commitment to TQI phase 2, 'Making it happen'. Of particular importance is the commitment being made at each session with reference to the way forward, and how the teams will continue to be supported in the resolution of their problems.
- The emphasis on team recognition and publicity.

Team recognition and publicity take numerous forms:

- The presentation of successful problem resolution by discussion groups and quality action teams to the Rover Group board and visiting companies/ organizations.
- Annual discussion group get-togethers, inviting discussion group members and their partners to an evening symposium which includes fixed displays by each group of their achievements throughout the year, a meal and two presentations by discussion groups about the resolution of a particular problem. *Land Rover News* regularly covers this event and the evening is attended by Rover Group board members, business unit directors and senior management.
- The building of the education partnership centre for the purpose of opening up the facilities for the development and education of schoolchildren and students of all ages.
- The belief that total quality is not just for the motor industry but for everybody. Land Rover therefore welcomes and encourages other companies, education authorities and health authorities to visit the company and share its experiences in implementing a total quality improvement programme. This extends into the help given to the establishment of the local training and enterprise council and presenting TQI papers at conferences.
- Stopping the track when a problem exists is now encouraged in order to ensure that right first time is achieved. The restart is allowed only after either an engineering concession is provided to give assurance that the concern will not affect either vehicle quality or reliability, or another suitable action is agreed.

Management commitment extends beyond improving the product to the quality of employee working life. Improvements in the environment, working conditions, amenity areas and health and safety have been made, and the employees' well-being is catered for with some innovative ideas:

- Healthy eating menus in the restaurant.
- Keep-fit sessions for employees after work.
- Aerobics.
- Callisthenics.
- Audiometry tests.
- Fitness screening and health advice.
- Chiropody service.
- Voluntary medical insurance scheme.
- Retirement/pension counselling.

- Provision of a crèche called Nurseryland, offering a valuable service to parents of young children.

Management commitment to quality improvement cannot rest with just the internal organization. In a company of Land Rover's size, there is a great deal of reliance on both suppliers and the dealer organization to be as committed to total quality as Land Rover is. A conscious initial decision was made not to involve suppliers and dealers (other than in the diagnostic stage of understanding Land Rover's own failings) until it could demonstrate its commitment to quality improvement and show how effective the process was.

Dealers

As a result of the company's experience, a programme was developed in 1991 called total customer satisfaction (TCS). While external consultants have been involved, the company has also used its own people as a resource: for example, 11 managers were trained to deliver the programme to all Land Rover commercial staff. The directors and managers were then required to help the process by attending and supporting the delivery to the dealer principals and management workshops.

Suppliers

A different approach was used here. Rover Group has established a new standard, RG 2000, for all suppliers to comply with. RG 2000 has been designed to define *minimum* requirements. The standard emphasizes strategic issues which are often overlooked, and encourages both ownership and flexibility in achieving common goals.

In addition to requiring suppliers to achieve accreditation to BS 5750, Rover Group will be assessing suppliers' attitudes towards employees and to the philosophy of total quality. The publication of RG 2000 is an acknowledgement by Rover Group that it needs to form long-lasting partnerships with suppliers to maintain successful, competitive businesses into the next century.

In support of this, all the company's suppliers have received an RG 2000 pack which consists of brochures covering the following areas:

- Supplier business specification.
- Best practice with suppliers.
- Supplier component status report.
- Total quality improvement.
- A 25-minute video.

The total quality improvement brochure is an overview of how Land Rover incorporated TQI, clearly identifying that the company was looking for its suppliers to implement similar total quality improvement programmes, with Land Rover's help if required.

Supporting recognition of achievement

Recognition of achievement activities include the following:

- Suggestion scheme payments.
- Personalized ways of saying 'thank you' implemented by functional directors, e.g. company vehicle for the weekend, barbecues and 4 × 4 cross-country activities at weekends.
- There is also a house newspaper *Land Rover News* and the *Group TQI News*, where both group and individual achievements can be published.
- A special Internal Supplier of the Year competition, where employees submitted the names of colleagues who had provided them with an extra special service.

One of the strategic initiatives for 1990/1 was to reduce the cost of quality across Rover Group by £100 million, with each of the sites being given a target to aim for. Quality action teams were set up across the company with champions being appointed at each site to maintain the focus and act as a catalyst. It was an overwhelming success, with an £89.4 million saving being achieved by the end of 1990.

In recognition of the hard work and effort put in by the teams, a recognition lunch was organized in the Metropole Hotel at the National Exhibition Centre. It was not just a 'thank you' dinner for the 850 attendees; it included displays of the actions that people had taken, plus a presentation by Bill Conway, one of the 'quality gurus' of the western world.

During 1991 it was recognized that this was not sufficient. With the increase in teamwork and the achievements of all the workforce, a more structured recognition system was needed. What was really needed was to recognize employees' involvement. Not all employees are geniuses and inventors, and not all are necessarily in a working environment which enables or fosters creative thinking. Therefore two recognition award programmes were developed which not only recognize the consistent loyal stalwarts who constantly do their job, but also cater for the outgoing, energetic or dynamic employee who wants to be involved in everything.

The excellence award

This is given as a result of differing levels of outstanding contribution to quality and comes from being nominated by a customer or supplier, either internally or externally. There is no monetary reward, but recognition takes the form of a certificate or ultimately a trophy (silver or gold). The latter is an accolade recognized by all as representing an outstanding contribution to quality, and it can be awarded to an individual or a team. Each and every award winner's achievement is recorded in a quality excellence register, and names are included on a roll of honour for public display.

RISE (recognition of involvement scheme for employees)

This has been developed to recognize people's involvement in and continuous contribution to the improvement processes within Land Rover. The scheme operates on a points system – points being awarded for participating in discussion groups, quality action teams, and the suggestion scheme. In addition, the successful resolution of a problem and taking part in a formal presentation about an achievement to external visitors, directors or other special functions earns a higher level of points. The points accumulate and provide significant levels of reward, the ultimate being a brand new Rover car and a holiday in America.

LESSONS AND IMPLICATIONS FOR THE FUTURE

TQI lessons

Land Rover has learnt many things from the experience of implementing a total quality improvement strategy, and some of these are shown in Figure 5.7.

- Never assume, always measure.
  - Viewpoint 1992 comparison with 1990:
  1. Better leadership
  2. Improved communications.
  3. More emphasis on quality.
  4. Improved image.
  5. More personal involvement.
  6. More effective working.
  7. More challenging work.
  8. Better working conditions.
  9. More learning opportunities.

- Effect of role model (management lead).
  - Introduction of workwear.

- Desire to involve everybody.
  - We focused initially on number of people trained.
  - Should have measured the opportunities in the workplace.
  Cannot emphasize enough. ESTABLISH LOCAL OWNERSHIP.

- Do not confuse people with initiatives which do not fit under the TQI banner.

Figure 5.7 TQI lessons

The company expects to build on this knowledge base and to continue to develop quality improvement into the future.

Future plans for quality improvement

The Rover Group has, over the last two years, closely analysed the Rover business processes. The complete Rover process was then divided into nine key business processes:

- New product introduction.
- Manufacture.
- Logistics.
- Maintenance of facilities and equipment.
- Sales and service.
- Corporate learning.
- Management of people.
- Product improvement.
- Business planning.

During 1991 approximately 700 people in all functions were involved in a process to identify a set of milestones for each key business process. In this context, a milestone is an action or an event which can be objectively verified and which will make a significant contribution to the quality of the process. The quality strategy has been produced on behalf of the Rover Group quality council, all of its members fully approving its contents.

During 1991 the quality strategy was incorporated in the business planning cycle, and it is now reflected in function and business unit plans for 1992 and beyond. Detailed action in support of the quality strategy is incorporated in current management objectives, which will remain the focus for management actions. In 1992 achievement of the milestones was advanced through the business review process and by further consultation exercises.

Within the Land Rover business unit, six critical success factors (CSFs) have been identified, both supporting the quality strategy and reinforcing a commitment to providing 'extraordinary customer satisfaction' (Figure 5.8) Against each CSF, cham-

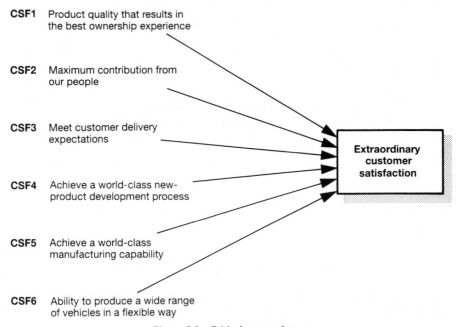

CSF1   Product quality that results in
the best ownership experience

CSF2   Maximum contribution from
our people

CSF3   Meet customer delivery
expectations

CSF4   Achieve a world-class new-
product development process

CSF5   Achieve a world-class
manufacturing capability

CSF6   Ability to produce a wide range
of vehicles in a flexible way

**Extraordinary
customer
satisfaction**

Figure 5.8   Critical success factors

pions have been appointed at director level who have identified key measures to be benchmarked, plus other measures. In many instances, action plans have been put into place for monitoring improvement trends.

Land Rover Powertrain has also established CSFs, and has undertaken a quality functional deployment (QFD) matrix against the identified requirements for its functions. The matrix lists the CSFs and ranks the action in order of priority. As with Land Rover Vehicles, Land Rover Powertrain has also established a set of measures for review.

Future plans for employee involvement

Quality improvement, not only of the product, but of the environment and the workplace, will be assisted by the increase and development of discussion groups and the improvements which will come from the quality action teams. A number of training initiatives have been identified to continue through 1993 and beyond.

For example, Land Rover Powertrain has planned future training for all its manufacturing employees. Powertrain engineering has identified many more modules as a result of the wide range of topics on which training has been requested, and thus extra options have been provided. In addition, there are a further five initiatives (set out below) intended to come on stream during 1992.

TQI phase 2 – 'Making it happen'

During 1991 the company identified the need to maintain the TQI impetus. Following surveys of the functions, it developed the TQI phase 2 programme. Figure 5.9 outlines the TQI training programme planned through to 1993.

	Start	Finish
Phase 1		
A) 750 directors and managers	April 1989	September 1989
B) 750 supervision	September 1989	January 1990
C) 6,800 staff and hourly paid employees	March 1990	December 1991
Phase 2		
A) 6,000 associates	June 1992	April 1993 (target)
B) 800 technical associates	September 1992	April 1993 (target)
Quality action teams		
Training/development of teams	November 1990	December 1992
Dealer training (Bespoke)	September 1992	Ongoing
Supplier involvement		
RG 2000	September 1992	Ongoing
Joint supplier quality action team training	September 1992	Ongoing
Total customer satisfaction programme with dealers		
130 dealers	September 1991	September 1992

Figure 5.9   The TQI training programme

Additional coaching has been provided in the following areas:

- Brainstorming.
- Cause and effect diagrams.
- Paired comparisons (consensus reaching).
- Flow charting.
- Introduction of measurement and presentation of data.

Over 107 advisers have been trained for the delivery of the phase 2 programme, which commenced in February 1992.

The structure places considerable emphasis on the team. Instead of having cross-functional groups, the company is putting together two work groups, six from each cell (a total of 12), with their own manager/facilitator or team leader being the adviser. Apart from the team-building aspect, part of the course concentrates on problem solving. Each cell selects a problem it is experiencing, applies the tools and techniques to scope the causes, and finishes by highlighting four or five possible causes which the team takes away to look at in more detail. The groups then reconvene at agreed times to review their progress.

Competitive benchmarking (CB)

Developed by Rover Group central quality and piloted during 1991, it has been found that competitive benchmarking plays an important role in corporate strategy formulation and is linked to the CSF key measures referred to earlier.

Competitive benchmarking is defined as 'the continuous process of measuring our products, service and practice against the toughest competitors or those companies recognized as the leaders'. The process features five key stages, shown in Figure 5.10,

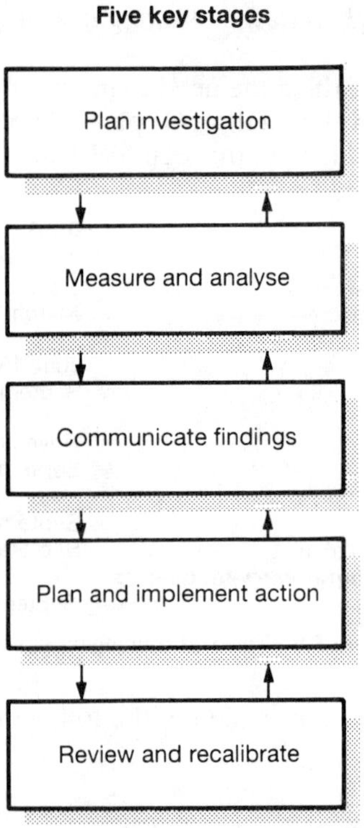

Five key stages

```
        ┌─────────────────────────┐
        │   Plan investigation     │
        └─────────────────────────┘
              │              ↑
              ↓              │
        ┌─────────────────────────┐
        │   Measure and analyse    │
        └─────────────────────────┘
              │              ↑
              ↓              │
        ┌─────────────────────────┐
        │  Communicate findings    │
        └─────────────────────────┘
              │              ↑
              ↓              │
        ┌─────────────────────────┐
        │ Plan and implement action│
        └─────────────────────────┘
              │              ↑
              ↓              │
        ┌─────────────────────────┐
        │  Review and recalibrate  │
        └─────────────────────────┘
```

Figure 5.10   Competitive benchmarking

which provide a framework to foster a common Rover approach to the crucial aspect of business analysis. Training is available for CB sponsors and team members, and 'experts' are available across the Rover Group sites to help coach the teams.

The goal of CB is to achieve and then maintain competitor advantage. This structured learning activity must be a continuous process. Integral to the approach, therefore, is a review phase involving recalibration of benchmarking targets to meet future needs.

Quality delivery process (QDP)

During 1992 this process was developed as the means to enable managers and technical staff areas to integrate total quality with normal business routines in a systematic manner. The QDP enables managers and work groups to clarify their purpose and objectives, to understand the needs of their internal customers and suppliers, and to organize and measure their activities in such a way as to promote continuous improvement in performance.

There are 10 steps in the QDP with the objective of delivering quality work in everyday activity. It focuses on the natural work group and progresses through three phases:

1. Mission and output review (steps 1–3).
2. Output standards from customer requirements (steps 5–7).
3. Quality action planning and measurement (steps 8–10).

Team strategy for work assignments

The motor vehicle business has always had to be flexible in its build schedules in order to meet demand and/or specification changes. These changes usually resulted in main assignments changing and in operators having to learn new skills. Quality has traditionally suffered owing to production line rate changes.

Towards the end of 1991 Land Rover piloted the introduction of team strategy, which provides the opportunity to develop a method of introducing a production line rate change which will protect quality levels. The team strategy concept introduces a stabilizing effect:

- Work will now remain stationary on the production line.
- The team will remain the same.
- Work will only be moved between members of the team.

This measure also supports improvement as the operators within the team are trained to do the work allocated within that team. Since the team is a group of people who have to work with each other, they are the customers and suppliers of each other and should be able to decide among themselves which work elements or tasks best suit each operator. Consequently, each team now receives a team assignment and decides on when and where the work will be done within the team.

The success of the pilot led to the implementation of the team concept throughout the Land Rover Vehicle assembly area in 1992, with training and support being provided by the vehicle assembly conformance department. Team assigning is another step in working towards total quality.

Personal development files (PDFs)

The PDF has been developed by the Rover Learning Business as a lifelong record of learning development and achievement, whether internally or externally recognized, and it provides the opportunity for individuals to develop as far as they want to go.

Working with their 'manager' (the term 'manager' is used throughout the PDF to denote managers, supervisors, team leaders, facilitators or any other person responsible for the development of others), individuals are able to work out and develop a programme of learning which meets their specific requirements. The development process is shown in Figure 5.11 and has cascaded down from the directors through management to the associate level. Training has been given to the directors and their

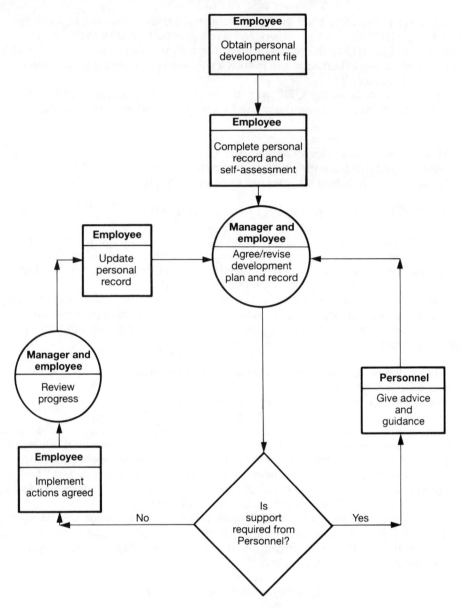

Figure 5.11 The development process

first line in how to cascade the PDF opportunity to their employees, and they have also been coached in the assessment process and review.

The personal development file contains the following items:

- Personal development plan.
- Local workplace information.
- Certificates of achievement – external.

- Certificates of achievement – internal.
- Personal records.

These are all contained within a hard plastic case.

Rover tomorrow – today

The new single-status working practices, which have been agreed in principle with the unions after many meetings of joint working parties, are possibly the most significant step change towards the implementation of total quality that Land Rover will ever make. The main features of this agreement are as follows:

- No clocking.
- Single status.
- Flexibility of labour.
- Flexible holidays.
- Revised sick pay arrangements.
- Company workwear worn by all.
- Free company-provided health checks.
- Enhanced focus on training.
- Greater emphasis on involvement.

Changes will be made in consultation with the trade unions and associates so that they can be introduced in a planned and orderly way. There is also a very ambitious programme of capital expenditure to improve facilities in order to give employees a better opportunity of building vehicles right first time.

Employees are the most important asset of the company, and future plans, as described in some detail in this chapter, emphasize that Land Rover wishes its employees to be totally involved in the business, and to be party to the discussion required to bring about the achievement of the corporate vision: to ensure that 'Rover is internationally renowned for extraordinary customer satisfaction'.

PRUDENTIAL ASSURANCE:
The 'Way of Life' programme

SALLY MESSENGER
AND
STEPHEN TANNER

SIX

Prudential Assurance:
The 'Way of Life' programme

INTRODUCTION

The aim of this chapter is to provide an analysis of the 'Way of Life' (WoL) quality improvement programme which was introduced by the Life Administration Board of Prudential Assurance in May 1989. The chapter begins by providing an overview of the company and the events which led Life Administration to develop a total quality management (TQM) system. The planning process involved in the development of the Way of Life programme is explained and there is a description of the four-point quality strategy that evolved. An important part of any quality improvement programme is the degree of management commitment given to the project, and this is identified along with the rewards system developed for employees with quality improvement ideas. The next section focuses on how the TQM programme is measured, controlled and reviewed. The level of training provided to support the Way of Life project is explained, and subsequent training courses are detailed. Participation is vital for the success of the TQM initiative, and the ways in which Life Administration attempted to achieve this are explored. The chapter then moves on to look at two examples of innovations which evolved from the Way of Life initiative, and this is followed by a review of the implications of the Way of Life programme and a look into the future of quality improvement at Prudential.

PRUDENTIAL ASSURANCE

Prudential Corporation plc is one of the world's largest and strongest financial services groups with more than eight million customers. Its main businesses are life assurance and pensions, general insurance, life and general reinsurance, and investment management. The Prudential was established in 1848 and in Victorian Britain the company succeeded because of its reputation for security and integrity. The key symbol of these unchanged criteria is the figure of Prudence representing the cardinal virtue of practical wisdom.

Since its formation in 1848, the 'Prudential Investment, Loan and Assurance Association' has evolved and developed. The key stages in Prudential's history are as follows: 1921 – First overseas office opened. 1968 – Company acquired majority holding in Mercantile and General Reinsurance. 1978 – Prudential Corporation formed as a holding company. 1985 – Purchase of first estate agency firm (withdrew from this in 1991). 1986 – Acquisition of Jackson National Life, USA, and launch of new corporate identity. 1991 – Premium income from long-term business exceeded £6 billion.

Prudential Corporation is divided into a number of business divisions which are illustrated in Figure 6.1. In the UK the organization is dominated by the Home

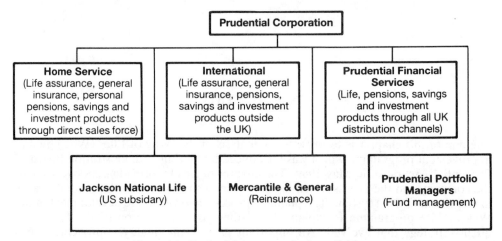

Figure 6.1 Prudential Assurance: business divisions

Service division, whose core products are life assurance, personal pensions and general insurance. The field force of some 13,000 local representatives are supported by Life Administration offices in Reading and Belfast where some 1,500 people work. The Reading office provides essential administrative back-up for new business, servicing accounts and claims for life and pensions business. The scale of the operation is illustrated by the fact that in 1991 15 million contract records existed and that on average 100,000 new proposals are processed each month.

As a long-established company, Prudential had well-developed systems and procedures which had met the needs of the business in its early years when the market was less competitive and customers were less demanding. In the late 1980s a number of changes occurred which led the Home Service division to review its position and to develop a new approach to its business. One significant change concerned the number of companies entering the financial services industry. Prudential had always enjoyed a position of rising profits but had not recognized that its market share was declining. As a large company with a long history, the Prudential had not considered itself to be vulnerable and to a certain extent was unaware of the external environment and its impact on its activities.

A second change which was to have a significant effect on the business was the introduction of legislation concerning the personal pension market. The years 1988 and 1989 represented a watershed for Prudential as it successfully gained a large part of the new pension business. The unexpected growth placed pressure on the company to recruit 500 new staff over a period of two years and to train them very quickly to perform specific tasks. This immense period of activity altered patterns of work and in essence acted as a catalyst for change.

Simply to maintain its position in the market place, Prudential needed to change – to re-establish dominance required a radical appraisal of processes and thinking. While the need for change was becoming clear, the strategy still had to be developed. A holistic approach focusing on customer requirements was to be the way forward for the Prudential.

Deregulation and increasingly sophisticated clients forced all financial sector companies to evaluate their operations critically. Clients expected an ever-improving service and even long-established corporations could no longer rely on reputation only. Without repeat business and customer recommendations, the survival of companies could not be assured. Those organizations not meeting client expectation would slowly lose their share of the financial services market.

Modern customers demand suppliers to be dynamic and flexible, but to retain the best aspects of tradition and reputation. They must be able to make major change quickly without compromising quality of service or value. Prudential needed to become totally customer focused, knowing exactly who its customers were and precisely what they wanted at all times.

DESIGN OF THE QUALITY IMPROVEMENT PROGRAMME

In May 1989 the Life Administration business plan defined key business targets and activities to be undertaken over a three-year time frame (1990–2). Extensive market research was undertaken as part of the planning process and two main conclusions were drawn:

- Life Administration's productivity had to increase if its policy-holders were to receive first-class returns on their investments. Market trends indicated that the current staffing levels could not be supported.
- Customers wanted a speedy service, delivered in a friendly but professional way at a cost that allowed excellent returns. While Prudential was seen as good, it was not considered the best. This perception had to change.

As a result of undertaking the market research project, the decision was taken to implement a total quality management (TQM) programme, which subsequently became known as the 'Way of Life'. Productivity improvements flowing from a quality-driven culture were seen as the solution.

The managing director of Life Administration, Tony Freeman, had a simple vision for the future of Prudential: 'to be the best provider of high-quality, low-cost financial services'. His views were supported by the head of Life Administration, Kippa Alliston, who demanded: 'customers should receive 100 per cent service from us, not just most of the time but all of the time'.

It was recognized that, to make this vision a reality, the culture of Life Administration needed fundamental change. Business targets in themselves would focus attention on costs and increase individual efforts, but this would not be sufficient to bring about the degree of change desired. Life Administration had to organize itself in a way that mirrored customer needs and encouraged staff to work together, speaking a common language that would spread the quality message. The aim was to create an environment and culture that would facilitate the required change and then embed it in the fabric of Life Administration operations.

The success of leading companies is significantly attributed to the enforcement of quality and continuous improvement cultures. The role of quality is witnessed by the increasing number of major awards presented in recognition of business service excellence both in the UK and internationally. To be a major player in the future, Prudential needed to be at the forefront of the UK quality movement.

THE QUALITY IMPROVEMENT STRATEGY

In order to implement a successful TQM programme, Life Administration needed to make a significant number of changes and to invest a large sum of money. It was, therefore, essential that the approach selected suited the needs of Prudential.

Over a period of nine months, a team of senior line managers began planning the change programme, aware that they needed to involve all the staff and to identify relevant quality management tools and techniques. During this period a number of key decisions were taken to help manage and focus the process:

- Life Administration had the enthusiasm but not the expertise to formulate and deliver a successful TQM programme. Consultants would be needed.
- Ownership of the programme from the top to the bottom of the organization was vital. Generic training would be inappropriate.
- TQM on its own was not a full answer, but merely a first and important step. Other initiatives would be needed.
- The pace of the training would be critical – too quick would compromise the programme, too slow would lose impetus and focus.
- Concepts, tools and techniques needed to translate easily into the workplace, with the transition between theory and practice as seamless as possible.
- Materials and tools should be of the highest quality, very professional and user friendly.
- Management's commitment needed to be total, while progress would be measured and communicated to all.

The decision to develop and implement a TQM programme known as the 'Way of Life' (WoL) was taken. This was to be followed and strengthened by other major training initiatives and projects focusing on understanding and delivering total customer satisfaction. The original 'Way of Life' programme concentrated on the elimination of workplace problems.

Some quality programmes only tackle the culture, whereas others are designed to equip staff with the 'tools for the job'. The approach taken by Prudential was a mixture of the two. The emphasis during management training was on engaging a culture which accepted change, the 'soft issues'; and the focus for clerical grade training was one of activity and implementation of solutions, the 'hard issues'. This mixture of hard and soft issues was the theme which ran throughout the WoL training. The main objectives of the training were to increase productivity and meet customer requirements. These were summarized under hard and soft categories (Figure 6.2).

Soft	Hard
• To change the way people behave.	• To improve accuracy.
• To reinvigorate the organization.	• To improve speed.
• To introduce a common language.	• To meet customer expectations.
• To get everybody involved.	• To reduce costs.
• To increase customer focus.	• To improve morale.

Figure 6.2 Soft and hard objectives

The quality initiative and business plan objectives were seen as indivisible. The three-year business plan set targets for accuracy, speed, customer satisfaction, morale and productivity. The 1992 target for speed, for example, was to achieve a five-day turnaround for all processable transactions. The training was aimed at providing the tools and techniques to all staff so that they could get involved in improvement activities which would lead to the achievement of these targets.

Although the messages contained in the training were similar, different approaches were taken at different levels of the organization. Management's key role was to evolve a culture that enabled change. This was the first stage of the training. At the clerical level, where the scope for influencing the direction of the organization is limited, the key emphasis was on positive involvement in quality improvement activity. This was the prime objective of the third stage of the training.

In addition to taking the WoL decision, the team of managers acting as facilitators to plan and support the quality initiative developed the Life Administration mission statement: 'We administer Prudential Assurance Life business. Our purpose is to delight our customers by delivering a quality service, in a cost-effective manner, through the contribution of everyone.'

Quite often, a company has a top-level mission, but nothing to support its implementation. In order to avoid this situation occurring, Prudential developed a set of 'principles and values' which translated the words contained in the mission statement into points which were easy to understand and described the culture they were trying to develop within Life Administration. These points became known as the Way of Life statements (Figure 6.3).

To assist the cultural change and to help Life Administration meet its performance targets, a four-point quality strategy was developed.

- *Control of processes* Getting processes 'right first time' and having an understanding of their interdependency. Service excellence can be delivered only through capable processes.

- *Customer-focused culture* Listening to customers and reacting quickly to their changing requirements – basically, doing the right things.

- *Continuous improvement* Adopting continuous improvement as a strategic imperative and striving to exceed customer expectations. Within this segment of

Our way of life

We are committed to delivering a quality service to our customers:
- The customer is the reason we exist and the key consideration in carrying out our day-to-day business.
- The customer is the person or area to whom we are providing a service.
- Everyone is a vital link in the service chain, and the successful partnership between the suppliers of services and their customers is of primary importance.
- As individuals and teams we demonstrate our commitment to our customers by 'getting it right first time'.
- We will continually review, redefine and improve the quality of service we provide to meet the changing expectations of our customers.

We recognize that our purpose can only be achieved through people:
- We recognize that everyone wants to provide a quality service.
- Each individual has the right to know what is expected of them and the reasons why.
- We are committed to providing continuous education, training and development opportunities to enable everyone to realize their full potential.
- Each individual is responsible for providing a quality service.
- We encourage people throughout the organization to listen actively to each other and to voice their ideas and opinions.

We are committed to creating a business-like and caring working environment:
- We will communicate in an open manner, which mirrors and supports our Way of Life.
- Teamwork will play a vital part in achieving our purpose.
- Opportunity will be given to individuals and teams to make changes at the level where it is most practical.
- We actively support the local community and the wider environment in which we live and work.

Figure 6.3   Way of Life statements

the quality strategy there are six areas: leadership; improvement activity; education; measurement and benchmarking; reward; and recognition and continuance.

- *Communication*   Keeping everyone in touch and promoting TQM within both Life Administration and Prudential in general. This involved upward, downward and horizontal communication.

VISIBLE MANAGEMENT COMMITMENT TO THE PROGRAMME

Instead of placing emphasis on controlling people, which had been the hallmark of management since the 1950s, Life Administration management developed a style based on effective leadership and total quality management. Lack of management commitment is often cited as the reason why quality programmes fail.

Within Life Administration there is no defined strategy for displaying management commitment, but there is a blend of management style that works. For example, management champion the cause and participate, and, very importantly, they listen. It was the board itself that sponsored the TQM programme. Senior experienced middle managers were assigned to the project team to facilitate the programme.

The Life Administration board was involved in establishing the mission statement, quality policy and 'principles and values' statements which describe the culture to which the organization aspires. They were also the first members of staff to be trained and the first to become involved with quality improvement activity.

Such was the commitment from the senior management that the training alone represented an investment of over 4,000 staff-days across all of the group.

Even though the original Way of Life programme was a major success, management were not complacent; they became more involved in the follow-up project 'Serving Customers – Our Way of Life'. The way this second programme was developed demonstrated management commitment. After the programme had been designed, a pre-pilot course was operated with the top 30 managers as delegates. Because of their determination to produce a successful programme, it was not allowed to run until it was felt that it met the needs of the business. The managers at board level taught the half-day business awareness modules that were delivered to all staff, to introduce the two-day 'serving customers' programme and to outline the business imperative for change. They also participated in discussions with staff during the sessions and took on board the 'live with' barriers to customer service that staff were not able to action themselves. In 1992 the programme ran over 50 times.

The structure project was another example of management commitment to quality improvement. Previously, departments were structured in a functional manner by product and type of transaction. This proved to be a major barrier to customer service, since staff were transaction focused. Often, several departments needed to contribute to a customer response, which became delayed and sometimes uncoordinated. To overcome this problem the board commissioned a complete review of the management and operational structure. A layer of management was eliminated, improving the command and communication chain. Products and transactions are now combined into divisional groups which provide the major customer, the field staff, with clear lines of access.

Restructuring led to the complete redesign of management roles and the definition of required competences, against which 150 staff were measured. With the new management structure in place, attention has been focused on reviewing the clerical roles. The aim has been to develop a closer relationship between multi-skilled groups of staff providing a comprehensive service to specific district offices.

Recognition of achievements

While an annual appraisal scheme was already in existence, the time frame was considered too wide for rewarding employees who developed quality improvement ideas. As a result the Way of Life award scheme was introduced.

This scheme has three levels of recognition: bronze, silver and gold. Bronze awards are considered by peers and are controlled by the quality management teams. To obtain a higher-value award, a presentation has to be given to the senior management team. This body either confirms the bronze, recommends a silver, or refers the achievement to the Life Administration board. The decision is then made as to whether the award should be bronze, silver or gold. Senior management's involvement in the award process is another visible sign of their commitment.

Senior management have supported quality improvement in many other ways. For example, senior management have delivered papers at international conferences on quality within Prudential. They have promoted quality within Prudential itself, with

Life Administration being viewed as a flagship. They have also supported staff attending conferences and meetings on quality, so that even junior members of staff can have the experience of learning from contact with other companies.

Finally, reference should be made to Life Administration being awarded the 1991 Northern Ireland Quality Award for service. A written report was submitted and this was followed by a site visit during which senior management and staff were interviewed for several hours. The significance of receiving the award was highlighted by the words of the judges: 'The award is granted for making rapid progress and achieving inspirational commitment from all managers and staff, so transforming an office working environment into a challenging and stimulating place to work.'

MEASUREMENT TO CONTROL AND ADJUST THE PROGRAMME

As the quality objectives are also the business objectives, the measurement systems for quality improvement throughout Life Administration are similar. There are some additional measurement systems which record quality improvement progress on a local scale, and the effectiveness of the quality improvement process itself is evaluated annually by way of an independent review.

Measurement throughout Life Administration

The five key business indicators (KBIs) and the way they are measured are summarized in Figure 6.4.

KBIs	Main measurement
Benefits to our customers:	
Attitude	Measured by quarterly customer satisfaction and one-month service-level agreement reviews
Speed	Measured by 4-weekly sampling at department
Accuracy	Measured by 4-weekly sampling at department
Benefit to Life Administration:	
Productivity	4-weekly productivity measuring and budget monitoring
Benefit to Life Administration staff:	
Morale	Monitored through annual employee surveys

Figure 6.4   Key business indicators

The main method used to monitor customer satisfaction is by reviewing the suppliers' performance against established 'service-level agreements' or SLAs for short. Monthly reviews are conducted to discuss performance.

Some areas also conduct internal customer satisfaction surveys.

The major customers, the field staff, fall into the internal customer category. A comprehensive quarterly customer satisfaction survey is conducted to assess the level of service that Life Administration is giving across various aspects of the business. There are three main line administration areas: Industrial Branch (IB) area, which has offices in Reading and Belfast, Ordinary Branch (OB) area and Personal Pensions (PP) area. Within these line areas, measurement is made against their performance on new business, servicing and claims, to name just three aspects.

Performance is also monitored through service-level agreements. This is done in a similar way to that described above for internal Life Administration customers.

Customer satisfaction is measured in three ways. All line departments keep a log of complaints. Great effort is put into resolving these complaints to the satisfaction of the policy-holder, and analysis is undertaken to look for trends so that preventative action can be taken.

A second way to monitor customer satisfaction is in the form of 'songs of praise'. These are letters which record a customer's appreciation of the service that has been provided. The number of songs of praise received is measured.

Finally, there is the work that Life Administration commissions through market research agencies. These agencies establish benchmarks for the industry against which the organization can measure itself.

Speed and accuracy

Staff, independent of the areas being measured, select samples from the high business volumes to measure both speed and accuracy. The same sampling techniques are used for the audits as they are the most effective given the volumes and current system technology. A major achievement during 1991 was the introduction, in a pilot area, of a new measurement system for speed. The system, based on a database called ACUMEN, counts all work that passes through the pensions new business area. Both volume and elapsed time are measured, and feedback is given to the area the following day. This allows for immediate analysis and corrective action when failures occur.

An important aspect of this new system is the detail of the data. Whereas the current sampling systems record elapsed time from the receipt of a proposal to the issue of a policy, the ACUMEN-based system breaks down the process and provides data at the various stages, i.e. proposal date to receipt in Reading, proposal receipt to acceptance, and proposal acceptance to issue of policy. Such detail reduces the process scope in the case of failure and makes for more effective corrective action.

Productivity

One measurement tool for productivity is budget monitoring. A management accounting reporting system (MARS) was introduced during 1991 which gave ownership of budget down to department level, whereas this was previously controlled at area level. Such ownership has allowed greater participation in the construction of the budget, with acceptance of budget restrictions imposed on Life Administration by the Prudential board.

Staff morale

An annual attitude survey is conducted across all of Life Administration. The results are analysed in terms of a communication index, a morale index, a training index and a service index. The results of the 1991 survey are shown in Table 6.1.

Table 6.1   Results of the 1991 attitude survey

Index	May 1991	Target
Communication	54	[50]
Morale	56	[50]
Training	55	[50]
Service	66	[50]

Team measures

The way the success of the quality improvement action is measured is by a subset of the business success criterion:

- *Customer impact*   An evaluation of whether the quality improvement action has had a 'major' or 'minor' positive impact on customers.

- *Time*   Staff in the early stages of the TQM programme did not think that they had time to work on quality improvement activities. Life Administration has therefore made 'time' a measure of success, to reinforce to staff that time spent on quality improvement activity is a profitable investment.

- *Money*   Direct cost savings in materials are evaluated.

- *Service*   If a quality improvement has a positive effect on either the accuracy or speed of the service, the improvement is classified in terms of a 'major' or a 'minor' effect.

- *Morale*   One of the benefits to staff of quality improvement is that removing quality problems makes their jobs 'hassle-free' and can remove some mundane tasks. Being listened to and having your idea implemented also gives greater job satisfaction.

Each team (or individual) evaluates the effectiveness of their improvement action when they close off their logged quality improvement initiative. The status of all the quality improvement initiatives, and benefits when closed, are recorded on team solution boards which are visibly displayed in the work areas.

Each four-week period, the quality management teams collate the data from the team solution boards all around their areas, and the total results across all of Life Administration are issued back to QMTs in a summary report. The figures also go to senior management for review.

Figure 6.5 shows the quarterly benefits from improvement action plus the totals for 1991. These results are very interesting as they show varying activity across all measures during the year.

Business results

The results for the speed and accuracy survey in 1990 and 1991 are shown in Figure

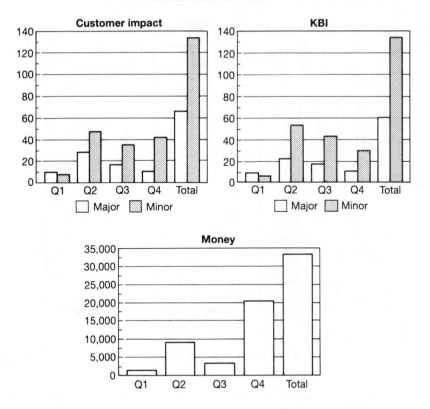

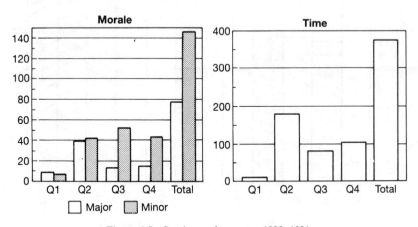

Figure 6.5 Service performance, 1990–1991

6.6. In the case of the speed figures, in 1990 the secondary target was 10 days and in 1991 it was 8 days.

For productivity, Figure 6.7 shows productivity improvement across the five IB areas. As IB, which deals with new business, is a function of the amount of new business received, the figure in January is higher than December.

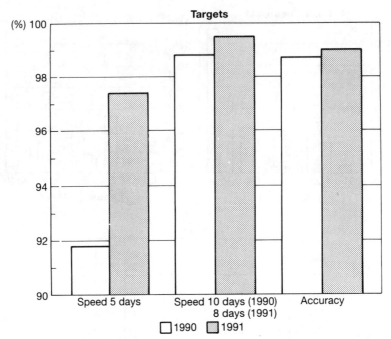

Figure 6.6   Industrial Branch productivity rates

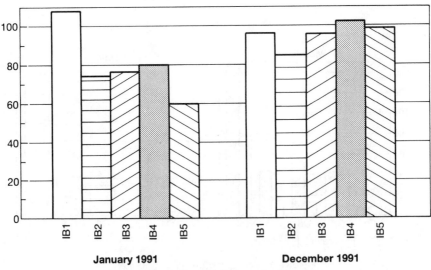

Figure 6.7   Ordinary Branch productivity rates

For the OB area, shown in Figure 6.8, the figures for the 10 departments which existed in January 1991 are compared with the figures for the 12 divisional departments. Here it is important to note the medians, which were 76.8 in January 1991 and 99.6 in December 1991.

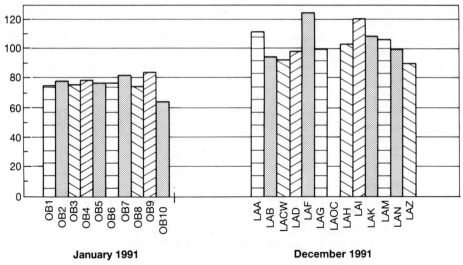

Figure 6.8 Benefits of improvement action, 1991

In addition to the productivity improvements, there have also been savings of £5 million in operation costs.

Way of Life review

A team of consultants reviewed the attitudes and behaviour of Life Administration staff at the start of the quality initiative training and this was repeated a year later. Results on a 1 to 10 scale are shown in Table 6.2.

Table 6.2 Staff attitudes to quality

	Nov. 1989	Nov. 1990
How serious is management about quality?	6	9
How serious do you think your staff are about quality?	5	8
How well do individual managers work together?	6	7
How well do departments work together?	5	8
How does the company rate on employee communication?	5	8
How would your subordinates rate you in taking quality seriously?	6	8

These independent results speak for themselves. The consultants concluded: 'The initiative has succeeded in bringing about substantial change in communication, behaviour and attitudes to quality throughout the organization. The process has been received with enthusiasm at all levels and as a result the environment for continuous improvement has been established.' Clearly, the training had established a climate for change and a desire to improve. There are now over 150 supervisor-led improvement teams which meet on a regular basis and are working on over 1,000 improvement ideas across Life Administration.

In November 1991 a second review was undertaken by a different team of consultants. The research was conducted on a group interview basis, with a brainstorming session to list employees' views on the way the TQM programme could be improved. A total of 119 people took part in the exercise, which included the Life Administration board itself. A total of 19 questions were addressed by the teams.

Figure 6.9 shows the results of the 19 questions answered during the questionnaire session of the review in ascending order. Scores are on a 1 (disagree) to 5 (agree) scale.

On the positive side, the review found the following:

- Way of Life was highly visible and accepted by staff.
- Most people interviewed had personally taken part in quality improvement activity during 1991.
- There was no shortage of ideas.
- Commitment to provide customer satisfaction was high.

On the negative side, though:

- Management involvement needed to be more visible.
- The same vision was not shared by everyone.
- Computer systems and work procedures needed to be improved.
- By focusing more on improvement activity which affected several departments, major improvements in service could be achieved.

Action has now been taken on the results of the review. For example, the 'Serving Customers – Our Way of Life' business awareness programme has addressed the concern over the shared vision.

Action

Measurement itself is not effective unless it leads to action. The main process for review and action is through the contact process. Each four-week period, a report is compiled listing all failures. This report includes corrective action plans. The contact report is discussed at board level. It gives board members the opportunity to discuss issues in their area in an open team environment. This can lead to offers of help from other areas, or ideas on the way to tackle a specific issue. The control process does not only concern itself with performance-related measures. It also covers areas such as customer satisfaction results, employee survey results and customer complaints. To ensure that staff are kept informed with both achievement and actions, the results of the contact process are cascaded through the team briefing network.

RELATED TRAINING PROVISION AT ALL LEVELS

Although Life Administration had always been involved with on-the-job training, total quality management training did not start until February 1990. It would be wrong

1. Everyone in the organization shares the same vision of quality.   2.38

2. Systems and procedures are up to date and reflect best practice with today's technology.   2.50

3. The management culture develops employee trust by personal involvement and visibility.   2.63

4. There are no barriers between internal departments.   2.67

5. People are recognized for their contribution and work well done.   2.80

6. We conduct regular surveys to determine customers' product and service expectations.   2.86

7. Generally decisions here are based on sound data with good input from my level.   2.87

8. Customer satisfaction measures are set and published regularly.   2.87

9. Employees feel confident that management will act upon employee initiatives.   3.00

10. Management deal promptly with issues for improvement according to resources available.   3.00

11. Management communication to all employees is regular and up to date.   3.33

12. Teamwork is very good here.   3.50

13. Training plans are prepared and implemented which are relevant to employee requirements.   3.68

14. Throughout the organization there is a commitment to meet internal and external customer requirements.   3.69

15. Target setting with measurement and publication of performance is normal practice.   3.90

16. I know and understand the mission statement and quality policy.   4.11

17. Employee participation in problem identification and solving is practical and encouraged.   4.16

18. I believe in generating ideas for continuous improvement.   4.46

19. I have personally participated in an improvement initiative in the past 12 months.   4.70

Figure 6.9   Results of employee questionnaire, November 1991

to claim that the major improvements achieved are only a result of the quality training. Many other training initiatives have played a part in the success of the organization, good examples being performance management and team building.

A hallmark of the training is that it is specific to Life Administration. It addresses key business needs for Life Administration, aiming to make the training programme interesting and even fun. For example, module 2 for the customer care programme is highly activity based, with 30 people in teams within a suitable area so that there is a lot of energy generated. Teams complete assignments then promenade around the area observing the results of other teams' efforts.

Way of Life (TQM) training

The Life Administration TQM programme was launched by educating all staff. The training was conducted in three stages. In the first stage, 260 staff from board member to supervisor were trained over a six-week period. This represented over 800 days of training, delivered during the period February 1990 to July 1990. The main objective of this training was to begin to change the culture and gain acceptance, at all levels of management, of the need to improve quality. This initial part of the training was delivered by senior line managers and was based on lectures, workshop sessions, activity in the workplace and progress review sessions. Stage two of the programme concentrated on preparing supervisors and trainers and was led by Prudential training staff, who placed an emphasis on learning by involvement. This provided the supervisors with team leadership skills and support. This part of the programme commenced in August 1990 and was completed in October 1990.

During stage three, supervisors delivered the training to the 1,600 clerical staff over an eight-week period. The training represented over 3,000 days and was completed in April 1991. The aim of these sessions was to develop teams working together to improve quality.

To achieve the main objective of sustained quality improvement activity, the training material was designed so that there was a 'seamless transition between learning and productive involvement'. It had to be flexible in physical design so that it could be used 'in the workplace', and had to allow for different learning speeds and styles of delivery. Work groups led by their supervisors selected a problem which affected them and took a week-by-week, structured approach to its elimination. In summary, the material consisted of a coloured workbook written in a language suitable for the audience, with A2-sized sheets contained in a transportable A2 binder which was the focal point of the team discussions and A2 worksheets for team activities. The original WoL programme was so successful that it won a 1991 National Training Award.

Written to the same exacting standards as the original Way of Life programme, 'Serving Customers – Our Way of Life' takes the organization a stage further. Whereas the focus during Way of Life was on the elimination of workplace problems, the focus of Serving Customers was on achieving outstanding customer service. The programme was in three modules.

Half-day business awareness sessions were given to all staff. The first session was presented by the head of Life Administration, who discussed the 1991 business results plus the vision for 1992 and beyond.

The second session was delivered by Dr Westwood from the Manchester Business School, who gave his own personal view of the outlook for the financial services industry. This session was designed to make staff aware of the business imperative to improve both productivity and service.

Finally, a serving Life Administration board member presented a more local view to the staff. The objective of these sessions was to share the vision for the future and to prepare staff for the next part of the programme.

During 1992 all staff attended a two-day module which gave them the opportunity to identify barriers to excellent customer service. The module started by discussing exactly what made good customer service and what made bad customer service. Examples were given of 'good companies' and 'bad companies'.

Although the programme was given to all staff, the version given to managers and supervisors had an additional section to enable them to 'lead' customer care. One key learning point consistent with the Way of Life theory was that good customer service can be delivered only with capable processes.

At the end of the programme, staff were committed to both group and individual improvement actions to remove the barrier. Barriers which were outside the group's control were accepted by senior management, and a feedback process was put in place so that staff knew what actions had been taken.

One of the problems with packaged training programmes is that they are very prescriptive. The view within Life Administration was that such prescription destroys innovation and personal ownership. Although this is true, a structured approach can have value in terms of direction.

The quality management team (QMT) training package was developed to give QMTs some gentle direction. It also provided refresher training in quality improvement tools, as one of the prime functions of the QMT is to provide support and consultancy.

INVOLVEMENT OF ALL MEMBERS OF THE ORGANIZATION

Participative teamwork within Life Administration was launched through the Way of Life education programme. The organization had to change, and to give the staff the tools so that they could change. This was the key to success.

There are four types of improvement activity within Life Administration:

- *Strategic projects* These are management led and sponsored by a Life Administration board member or other senior manager. The projects are aimed at fundamental change to work practices and will often have a significant effect on Life Administration's performance and effectiveness. Frequently, such projects involve major change or enhancements to computer systems.

- *Cross-departmental improvement teams* Groups are formed voluntarily when a quality improvement opportunity is identified in one area and action has to be taken in another. Such initiatives tend to be substantial and may affect up to 12 separate areas. The close co-operation and greater understanding fostered by such activity is an important spin-off benefit.

- *Work groups* Work groups meet regularly to identify and implement quality improvement opportunities within their work area.

- *Individual action* Individuals are encouraged to take action that will result in an improvement either in their personal performance or to their assigned processes.

The focus on quality improvement is kept by having quality improvement as a key objective written into everyone's objectives and accountabilities. This was necessary as it overcame what was the major obstacle to keeping quality improvement going – the conflict between improvement and work volumes. These problems have been minimized because the business measures are also the quality improvement measures, but it has still been a long education process getting people to understand that the way to achieve the business targets is by action and not just by working harder. People had to learn to work 'smarter', and they did this by eliminating the many problems they faced day in, day out.

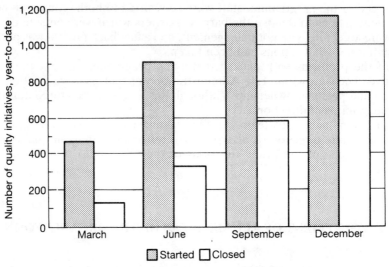

Figure 6.10   Way of Life work group activity, 1991

Figure 6.10 shows the progress that was made during 1991 in terms of the number of quality initiatives started and completed. But it has not all been plain sailing. One of the drawbacks of the education process was that the training was given to teams by their first line manager, and the effectiveness of the teams became a function of the competence of the first line managers in training them. Getting the first line manager to deliver the training ensured a high degree of line ownership for the quality process, made the training relevant on an area-by-area basis, and gave the first line managers some extra skills as part of the process. To support the first line managers in their roles, a support network was put into place to control the process and give advice. This network was, and still is, the quality management team (QMT) network, there being a QMT in each area.

The QMT structure in itself is a good example of teamwork in action. As mentioned above, each area has a QMT, and each QMT has a representative on the Way of Life Forum (WOLF). The WOLF has a responsibility to the Life Administration board, and WOLFs are always attended by at least one Life Administration board member.

When the QMTs were first established, they were chaired by the senior manager in the area and consisted only of area management. As these groups have evolved, a mixture of grades have been introduced into these teams and there are now teams consisting of senior management and clerical grade staff working together in order to achieve common objectives. This illustrates the major shift in culture that has taken place within Life Administration.

One final point to make on QMTs is that is is the QMT who award the first band of recognition in the Way of Life Award Scheme. So, there is peer recognition of people's achievements which is believed to be of extreme importance.

Many things fuel quality improvement. Problems or improvement opportunities are either identified through brainstorming sessions, or perhaps action is taken because an area failed a KBI target.

Problem identification and correction

Quality improvement is not made 'tool bound'. There are many examples where the only quality improvement action taken to solve a problem was people talking to each other to agree requirements. But during the Way of Life awareness training, all members of staff were taught how to use various tools and techniques in their quality improvement activity. They were also given a simple four-stage problem-solving process to follow, which was designed to solve problems permanently. This four-stage process was called 'DICE':

- *Define problem* There are six questions to be answered, which include defining the problem in a non-judgemental way, assessing its impact on the business and setting a success measure.

- *Immediate fix* The message was 'Do not pass on errors to your customer.' If some short-term action can be taken, it should be, unless it tampers with the process.

- *Corrective action on root cause* Problem-solving tools are used to establish the root cause of problems, and corrective action is taken to eliminate the root cause.

- *Evaluation* After the action has been taken, a period of evaluation follows to ensure that the root cause of the problem has been identified and eliminated. Benefit analysis also takes place within each stage.

This structured approach to problem solving is the basis of a combined tool which was called the QICPAC, which stands for Quality Improvement Cycle (Prudential Assurance Company). The QICPAC is just a summary of the material that was used during the original Way of Life awareness training given by the supervisors to their staff. It is now used by both teams and individuals. The pack includes improvement tools such as brainstorming sheets, measurement chart and action planning materials.

Some small changes were made to improve the material based on feedback from the staff, who were the customers of the QICPAC. The most significant change was that they no longer talk about 'Problems' but refer to 'Improvements', which includes problem solving and improvements. This change was made to encourage innovation. Figure 6.11 outlines the steps in the QICPAC.

Customer/supplier teams have also been established. For example, Life Administration staff work with their colleagues in field operations. It has been found that the staff can be more effective if they discuss quality subjects like proposal errors on the field staff's home ground. To this end they established several clinics where quality improvement and customer/supplier requirements are discussed.

Links have also been formed with other colleagues. For example, Life Adminis-

Step 1	Brainstorming sheet to select improvement.
Step 2	List the tasks to the process.
Step 3	Examine the process and requirements.
Step 4	Measure.
Step 5	Define improvement.
Step 6	Take immediate fix action if possible.
Step 7	Establish root cause.
Step 8	Plan and take action.
Step 9	Evaluate.
Step 10	Go back to step 1.

Figure 6.11   The content of QICPAC

tration works very closely with the computer systems area, which has an active TQM initiative itself. This collaboration has taken many forms. A 'Life User Group' has been formed so that Life Administration has an influence on the way in which computer systems projects are resourced. Life Administration also has a slice of the overall budget for Home Systems development and has a choice as to how that money is spent. In addition it reviews the 'value for money' aspects, which has provided a key driver for Home Service Systems in their own quality programme.

Computer system designers have introduced a process called the Home Service development life-cycle for the development of new systems. The process, which is a form of phased project management with clearly defined checkpoints, requires a high degree of user involvement as the customer joins a user group to establish true business needs. The process also includes a system implementation review, where the effectiveness of the development process is reviewed so that improvement action can be taken, if necessary. Three months after system implementation there is a post-development review, where the system itself is evaluated against the pre-defined business requirements. Life Administration takes part in both these reviews in the role of customer.

Innovation

To end this section, two initiatives on teamwork which took place in 1991 are detailed. These were the launch of independent pensions in January 1991 and the achievement of BS 5750 in the Industrial Branch in December 1991.

Launch of the independent pension project

When Prudential was planning to launch its independent pension product, Life Administration had to form a new department. Team members were chosen from the operations area to form a project team to plan for the launch of the product. What was different was that the team was both multi-disciplined and multi-levelled. In effect, management and clerical staff were working together to achieve the business objective in a non-grade-conscious environment.

There was a degree of ownership where clerical staff were allowed to challenge existing procedures and follow through their own ideas. Several innovative ideas were put into practice. For example, the clerical grade staff recommended that the normal practice of inspection should cease, and that they should take individual responsibility for the quality of their work. They were committed to getting it 'right first time'. They worked to design new processes which would achieve this.

In addition, in order that errors could be prevented and a better service given to customers, at their recommendation all team members were trained by the field staff training centre, so that they had detailed product knowledge. Life Administration staff took the same product test as the field staff sales representatives.

Before the time came to launch the product nationwide, extra staff were seconded into the unit and teams were trained and led by the core team members. The benefits of using this participative method of launching the product were that it was launched on time, the unit had lower staffing cost, the service they provided was higher both in terms of turnaround time and accuracy, and morale was very high because the department was working quality as a Way of Life.

BS 5750 registration

A key feature of the BS 5750 project was that registration was achieved in record time by using a team-based project method. Everybody in the area was a member of a team which was led by a junior clerical grade of staff. The team structure is shown in Figure 6.12.

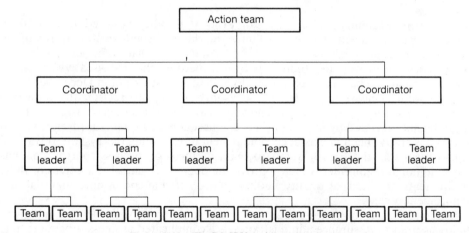

Figure 6.12 The BS 5750 action team structure

The action team was headed by the manager of the Industrial Branch administration area and consisted of all his departmental managers.

All the activity steps for the registration process were team activities led by the team leader. For example, the team leader gave the awareness training. The main steps of the process are shown in Figure 6.13.

By using a teamwork approach, total ownership of the quality system and procedures was achieved. What is more, people understood and accepted why registration was beneficial – they were part of the process. While the registration process was going on, it was not unusual to find teams working late at night and members taking their procedures home at weekends to work on them.

Apart from the obvious success of achieving registration, the project also improved morale and communications. In the words of one of the BSI assessors, 'we have never seen such total enthusiasm and commitment from all staff to achieving the goal of registration'.

Receptivity

↓

Awareness

↓

Sign up to goal

↓

Draft procedures

↓

Follow procedures

↓

Good practice

↓

Self-assessment

↓

Independent assessment

↓

BSI assessment

↓

Celebrate!

Figure 6.13　BSI registration process steps

There were no commercial pressures on Prudential to be registered to BS 5750. In addition, registration would have only limited marketing benefit as the majority of the policy-holders would not have heard of BS 5750 unless they had come across it in their own business. However, the Industrial Branch became the first area within an insurance company to be a registered firm, following an assessment in December 1991.

There were many reasons why the decision was taken to register the Industrial Branch area of Life Administration. The administration of assurance business is by its nature highly regulated by legislation. As a consequence, a quality assurance system of sorts has always been in existence. The benefit of extending this system to BS 5750 standard was that the British Standard, with its focus on process control, contains some additional requirements that improve the degree of control. Examples of these requirements are internal quality audits, control of non-conforming material and management review.

A second reason for seeking registration had more to do with the staff than with quality assurance. Assurance administration is a complicated business. For some time there had been an interest among staff in reviewing all the existing procedures and documentation which controlled the processes. The BS 5750 registration project provided a necessary focus on procedures so that this ambition could be realized.

A spin-off benefit of the work has been an improved consistency between the various departments within the Industrial Branch. For example, it has been found in the Belfast office that sometimes changes to similar processes in Reading were not being communicated.

REVIEW OF THE IMPLICATIONS OF THE PROGRAMME

The Way of Life programme has brought a number of benefits to Prudential. For example, the TQM initiative has sharpened the focus on forward planning activities and influenced the way Prudential manages its business. A significant change has been that staff are more proactive and more prepared to think about improving their work. The company has recognized that customers are becoming more discerning and that in the future 'service' will increasingly be the competitive edge for companies in the financial services sector. This drive to consider service as a vital element of the product has led Prudential to become customer focused – moving it away from its image as a procedure-dominated organization. Overall, the TQM programme has led to a more efficient business which prides itself on 'getting things right first time'.

Overcoming obstacles

A number of obstacles have been overcome since 1989 and lessons have been learnt. For some staff, the cultural shift that has taken place has been difficult to cope with and as a result they have left the organization. With any change there will be a degree of resistance from some individuals and it is very important that this is dealt with effectively by management. It is obviously much easier to introduce a TQM programme into a new or young business than into one which is restricted by many years of established procedures and tasks. As Prudential adopts its new culture, there will be implications for its recruitment policies and selection processes.

The time taken to 'roll out' a change programme is crucial – too quickly can mean that the details are not fully understood, and too slowly can result in a loss of momentum. The fact that some 1,800 staff received the same training meant that Prudential had to run the programme over a fairly long time span. The need to provide effective training materials was recognized early on, and much effort was invested in fulfilling this aim. Training staff is a sensitive task and attention needs to be given to ensuring that the 'pitch' of the material meets the requirements of the target audience and does not underestimate or overestimate their abilities. In addition, the language used must be meaningful and related to the particular needs of each department.

The TQM system having been launched, it is important that it is relatively straightforward to operate on a day-to-day basis. TQM, given its links with control and inspection, is often accompanied by bureaucracy in the shape of reports and form-filling exercises. At Prudential, while the TQM system was quite bureaucratic in the early stages, the paperwork was streamlined as staff became more confident with the new procedures. This is not an unusual situation; it is a learning process which all organizations have to go through.

When introducing a change such as the Way of Life programme, the change agent welcomes positive involvement from members of the organization. It is important, however, that this enthusiasm is harnessed to avoid too many initiatives being started at one time. While participation is to be praised, it is important that only those projects which are likely to bring benefits to the organization are supported – it is vital that effort and finances are not wasted.

In order to gain participation in the implementation of the change, management must demonstrate its support. This can be difficult when the change is likely to affect management roles. For example, at Prudential the establishment of working groups consisting of a cross-section of employees placed managers in a vulnerable position where they could be questioned and challenged by more junior members of staff. It is therefore very important that managers are well prepared for their role in the TQM system.

Issues for the future

Prudential is one of the first insurance companies to introduce a TQM system and as such it is 'breaking new ground'. A number of issues concerning the further development of TQM within Prudential are now being recognized. The first issue concerns the concept of TQM and the attention it has received. Within the organization, among some staff, there is the feeling that TQM is the 'flavour of the month' and that it has a limited life-cycle. Senior management realize that, having invested significant resources in developing the TQM system, they now need to ensure that it becomes totally integrated into the daily operation of the organization. Kippa Alliston has stated that TQM 'should be a change in the chemistry, not the drug'. In other words, the change in culture should be a 'Way of Life'.

Having developed and implemented a TQM system, Prudential now needs to review the structure and processes that have been put in place and wherever possible to make refinements and improvements. For example, one of the dangers in establishing a TQM system is installing too many working groups and teams. This can lead to confusion and a general lack of understanding about the total operation of the system.

Once a TQM system has been introduced into an organization, it is possible to concentrate on particular areas and to develop them further. One area that Prudential plans to concentrate on is making the customer-focus measures more quantitative. The speed and turnaround of policies are currently measured, but the intention is to look at this in more depth because Prudential realizes that customers will increasingly measure the company on the service it offers. The objectives of Prudential are now quality based, with success being measured in terms of customer satisfaction and not just input or cost. This represents a major shift in management approach.

Perhaps the most significant issue that Prudential now faces is: how does it maintain the momentum that it has generated, with regard to the development of TQM, throughout the organization? One of the benefits of the success that Life Administration has achieved with its Way of Life programme is the considerable interest that has been aroused in Prudential as a whole. This has raised the profile of TQM to the extent that the chief executive, Mick Newmarch, has declared TQM a strategic imperative for all the Prudential Corporation. The success of the quality initiative has also been promoted in several ways: for example, site visits are encouraged from other business areas to see TQM in action. During 1991 a forum was established within Prudential to discuss TQM. The meetings are called quality exchange days and are attended by representatives from throughout Prudential.

In addition to spreading the word about TQM throughout the company, there is a need to ensure that the initial enthusiasm generated at all levels of Life Administration is maintained. This means continually monitoring and reviewing the system and refreshing all members of the organization to ensure that the Way of Life concepts continue and adapt to the changing needs of the business.

Conclusion

Prudential has undoubtedly been very successful in bringing about a major change programme. Its success is perhaps best summed up in the words of the independent consultants who reviewed its progress along the TQM route: 'The Initiative has succeeded in bringing about substantial change in communication, behaviour and attitudes to quality throughout the organization. The process has been received with enthusiasm at all levels and as a result the environment for continuous change has been established.'

The success of the project has been proved in a number of ways. Internally, Prudential has met all its business targets and has frequently exceeded a number of them. Unit costs have declined while productivity has increased. This has been due to bringing work processes under control and ensuring that they are properly documented. Over the past three years the number of staff employed has been reduced by 300 as a direct result of the changes that have taken place. Customer satisfaction and morale indices show sustained improvement despite the many changes made by Life Administration in the way it organizes itself and does its work. It has been estimated that successfully implemented Way of Life initiatives saved, at a conservative estimate, over £1 million in the first full year of operation.

With regard to the external impact of its TQM programme, Prudential has won a number of major awards for its work. In 1991 the company received a National Training Award and the Northern Ireland Quality Award for Service. This was followed in 1992 by an award from the Institute of Administrative Management.

The quality initiative started life as a project designed to achieve the business objectives set in May 1989. After two years the training had been so effective that quality had been totally integrated into the business planning process and certification to the BS 5750 standard was on the horizon. During that time Prudential had become the leader in the area of TQM and, having achieved this position, it must now develop a strategy which maintains its place and keeps the company ahead of its competition.

GLOSSARY OF ABBREVIATIONS

KBI   Key business indicators. One way of judging a business is by identifying indicators and prescribing measurable targets for each.

QICPAC   Quality Improvement Cycle (Prudential Assurance Company). The material used during the original Way of Life awareness training.

QMT   Quality management teams. This represents a group of staff working together to achieve common objectives.

TQM   Total quality management system. This represents a package of measures designed to improve the quality of the service offered by Life Administration.

WoL   'Way of Life' quality programme which was introduced to resolve problems in Life Administration.

INDEX